A. Glenn Mandeville's
Madame Alexander Dolls
Value Guide

Published by Hobby House Press, Inc.
Grantsville, MD 21536

Dedication

This book is dedicated to all Madame Alexander doll collectors! Without their tireless hours of research, and appreciation of beauty, our knowledge of the legacy that Madame Alexander began, would not be possible.

Madame Alexander doll lovers come in all ages, sexes, sizes, and colors. They are as diverse and lovely as the dolls they collect! May you use this book to further increase your enjoyment of Madame Alexander dolls!

Acknowledgements

As with any project that involves in depth research and compilation, there are many wonderful and talented individuals that gave freely of their knowledge and time. The author would like to thank ALL who helped, and especially the following.

Bob Gantz, photographic assistance. Benita Schwartz, for the incredible listing of Alexander Store Specials. Joe Carrillo, for his help in editing price listings. Vivian Brady-Ashley, for her knowledge of rare Alexander dolls and values. Special thanks also go to Ann Tardie, Pat Burns, Marge and Earl Meisinger, Ann Rast, Neal Foster, Tanya McWhorter, Daun Fallon, Therese Stadelmeier, and Ira Smith, who is CEO of The Alexander Doll Company.

The author especially wants to notice Linda Collie, who gives me the time to undertake a project like this one!

Front Cover: Looking like the Queen she is, this 10in (25cm) hard plastic *Queen of Hearts*, was a limited edition of 500 pieces made just for the Disneyland Doll and Bear Convention, 1992.

Title Page: With a serene look and flowing gown, this all hard plastic 18" (46cm) Portrait doll is named *Pink Champagne* and dates from about 1950. Never shown in any catalog, she is unmarked with a tagged Madame Alexander gown. Another doll was purchased at R.H. Macy & Co. in a labeled box. *Neal Foster photograph.*

Back Cover: *Cissy*, #2017, 1956.

Additional copies of this book may be purchased at **$9.95** from
Hobby House Press, Inc.
1 Corporate Drive
Grantsville, Maryland 21536
1-800-554-1447
or from your favorite bookstore or dealer.
Please add $3.25 per copy for postage.

© 1994 by A. Glenn Mandeville

Printed in Canada

ISBN: 0-87588-406-7

Table of Contents

For three straight years in the early 1950s Madame Alexander won the prestigious Fashion Academy Award for Clothing Design. She is shown here in her office with three of her award-winning designs.

The Magic of Collecting Madame Alexander Dolls

There is indeed much magic, that elusive mystery and wonderment, that comes from just looking at a Madame Alexander doll. In my opinion, no other doll can come close to the quality, workmanship, and theme selection of the creations produced for over seventy years at The Alexander Doll Company.

During the "Golden Age" of collectible dolls, namely the late 1940s until the mid 1960s, Madame Alexander dolls were the standard by which all other dolls were judged.

It matters little if Madame was first with a new idea. When she entered the race, her version was always the best.

Some adult collectors recall memories of standing in front of well lit cabinets at "better" stores, and staring into the faces of the most beautiful dolls in all the world. Stores such as F.A.O. Schwarz, B. Altman, Lord and Taylor, Saks Fifth Avenue, and John Wanamaker could be counted on to have, safely tucked behind glass, floor to ceiling cabinets in which little pieces of perfection, haughtily gazed down on those who could afford such beauty. While true that Madame Alexander dolls cost much more than competitors' dolls, it was the quality and exquisite design that made Madame Alexander a legend.

The most often overlooked fact is that Madame Alexander was not a doll artist. She was a clothing designer, and won The Fashion Academy Award to clothing design three years straight in the early 1950s. More astonishing is that the competition was not just for doll clothing, but for ALL garments manufactured, period. This also was, and still is, a large part of the magic of Madame Alexander dolls. Each perfectly tailored little garment could be made for a miniature person. If you were only eight inches tall, you could have ballgowns, street wear, play clothes, and more. An entire realm could be your playground in your demure size. Everything from Peter Pan's bag of pixie dust, to Dorothy's red shoes would be in your imaginary closet!

Yes, the dolls themselves were rarely the star. The Alexander Doll Company tradition is to take a face, and use it to launch a thousand ships, something which they do quite well, and with great imagination. To Madame, the dolls, for the most part, were merely the mannequins upon which she draped her dreams, and her desire to educate those who would possess her creations.

Expensive, yes, and only available in "better" outlets, the dolls Madame created embodied her belief that today's child was not exposed enough to the great masters of art, literature, and culture. It was through her dolls, that notables such as Morisot, Renoir, Mary Cassatt, and others became familiar to those who purchased her dolls.

A life of culture, often neglected even in the educated, became real as the same little twelve inch doll became Lord Fauntleroy, Napolean and Josephine, Antony and Cleopatra, and even Rhett and Scarlett! One doll, one face, yet in the skillful hands of The Alexander Doll Company, magic WAS created as each new character came to life to thrill it's new owner.

Yes, there is magic in collecting Madame Alexander dolls. A collection of these perfect little miniature messengers of history and art, thrill and amaze all who see them.

For over seventy years, Madame Alexander and The Alexander Doll Company, are proving that a thing of beauty is truly a joy forever.

A 1966 *Scarlett* Portrait doll. Using the same mold as the *Coco* doll from that year, this *Scarlett* is the most valuable and magical of all the Portrait dolls. The *Coco* doll is regarded as the jewel in the crown of Madame Alexander dolls.

What IS My Alexander Doll Worth?

As a collector, dealer, and appraiser of dolls, the most frequent question I am asked when at shows, or by mail, is what is my Alexander doll worth?

The question, while seemingly simple can be compared to asking a stranger you meet "What is my car worth?" The person hearing the question would be shocked, as no further information is often given!

Some basic facts must be discussed. Antique dolls, defined as having a porcelain head, and over 75 years old, are evaluated quite differently than Madame Alexander dolls. This is where the most common mistakes can occur when buying and selling Madame Alexander dolls.

With an antique doll, the value is primarily in the head of the doll. The mold number, the facial expression, can add up to a doll head that is worth tens of thousands of dollars. The body can usually be "replaced" at a later date. "Period" clothing can always be found at a good doll show, and basically, the assigned value of the doll is contained from the neck up!

Madame Alexander dolls are another matter entirely. First, each doll is, almost without exception, like hundreds, even thousands of others. What makes the doll unique is the clothing, the wig, and the face painting. Thus a nude, wigless, Alexander doll has little, if any value, because the character of the doll is lost forever. Is it "Little Miss Muffet," or maybe "Oliver Twist"? Could the nude, wigless little creature be a boy or a girl; an adult or child?

The reader can quickly see that to bring top collector dollars, the doll must be complete, and with all accessories that it was sold with.

Secondly, the condition of the doll is almost all the value. The same collectors that stared lovingly at the doll cases in John Wanamaker's in Philadelphia, want that doll to look just as it did in 1957! After all, they remember it that way, and waited over thirty years to own it! Certainly they are not interested in used children's toys. They want, and are willing to pay for, perfection. The collector wants to cheat time, as it were, and pretend that it is Christmas morning, 1957, and they are opening their dream doll that they never really received!

With Alexander dolls, the seller must realize that the further you take the doll from crispy mint perfection, the lower the price goes. One has to understand that even in very rare dolls, the doll is either unplayed with, and mint condition, or it falls into the category of a used child's toy. Naturally, the played with doll has some value, often more sentimental than monetary, but the price drops drastically along with condition.

Factors which add to the value of an Alexander doll are, does the doll have original factory clothing, complete with all accessories? Is there a box? Does the doll have a booklet or wrist tag? Also factors such as a good facial coloring, and general eye appeal make for a superior doll.

There is much misunderstanding in the pricing of Alexander dolls. Some collectors will buy gently played with dolls and restore them, but they want the price to reflect the effort that they have to put forth to bring the doll up to another level. Other collectors simply will not look at a pale, badly played with doll, and regard it as something that should be discarded, or purchased for parts.

Sellers of dolls are becoming more educated to the fact that condition is the main ingredient in making an Alexander doll valuable. The dealer of today is more often a collector him/herself, and thus very in tune to the factors that make an Alexander doll valuable.

Another question that I am often asked, is that boxes of dolls are piling up all over the house, and what do I do? Many times a doll collector, myself included, loves EVERYTHING. Naturally, if space and money were not a consideration, I suppose this would not be a problem, but I can offer the collector my favorite ten tips to make your collection award winning!

Ten Tips to Make Your Collection Award Winning!

1. Decide on a focus for your collection. Try to stick to one particular size doll, or perhaps a theme such as fairy tale characters. The choices are endless! You could collect Dionne quintuplet dolls, bride dolls, the many versions of Scarlett, or nursery rhyme and international dolls. One enterprising gentleman in my area collects men and boy dolls, and has over 900 dolls! Another lady friend collects only dolls with red hair! By sticking to a category, you can avoid the "I have to have everything they make" anxiety, and strengthen your collection. What happens if you see an Alexander doll that is NOT in your category but you MUST have it? Well, like the person on a diet, you can splurge on that hot fudge sundae a few times, but not everyday!

2. Buy the best you can afford, and don't be afraid to upgrade if you see a better example. This is one area where you CAN be a bit obsessive! With older dolls, ask yourself if this doll is a better example than the one you have at home. Sometimes new dolls have fabric variations. If you see one you like better, buy it, and sell yours. The goal is always to have a strong collection in your chosen category.

3. If you are collecting a series, such as Americana dolls, or foreign lands figures, or anything similar, carry a small note book with you to doll shows. That way you will remember what it is you need to complete a certain grouping. Make a note of dolls you want to upgrade, as well.   *(continued)*

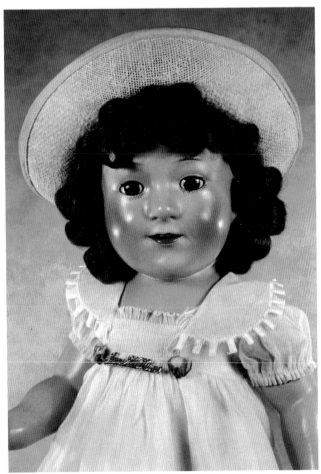

The prize of anyone's collection would be this stunning all composition *Jane Withers*. Complete with gold plated signature pin, she was made from a special doll mold. Her like new condition makes her a star!

4. Always note what accessories you need to make a doll go up a grade. Your notebook can list things like booklets, wrist tags, shoes, stockings, hats, etc., that can make a doll go from excellent to mint. It is possible to find these little things, I speak from experience, so note what it is you need.

5. Money is usually a factor with most collectors. If you see a doll at a show you need, inquire if the dealer has a lay-a-way policy. Credit cards, (a necessary evil in collecting), can be an option. When all else fails, at least get the name and phone number of the seller. Some dealers do only a couple of shows a year, and it IS possible that the item you are interested in will be available when you have the funds!

6. Assign each doll a code number. I use a letter code for the year, and a number for the item within that year. In other words, if 1993 is "A", then your first item is "1", making your code, "A-1". Use a small self-stick label, and put your code on the bottom of the doll's shoe. In a notebook, record the date of purchase, check number, receipt from the seller, etc. Get your collecting insured, and photograph your dolls. Keep this information in duplicate in a place off the premises such as a safe deposit box, or at a family member's home.

7. Enjoy your collection. Why have closets full of boxed dolls? Rotate a display around a holiday theme, or family tradition. Invest in built-in cabinets or curio cases. Having a doll out in the air for a month or so will not hurt it, and will give the material a chance to "breathe." Remember, there are only a few precautions you need to follow. Keep dolls out of direct sunlight, or even brightly lit areas, avoid dust by using cases, and keep dolls away from small children and pets. Dogs are attracted by the smell of plastic, it seems! I think it is better to risk a little wear and tear on your treasures, then have them all packed away. DO enjoy your purchases.

8. Read all you can on Alexander dolls. There are many excellent publications that can assist you. Company catalogs are in-valuable, but sometimes changes and variations do exist, as catalogs are often made up before the dolls are produced. They are a valuable research tool, but are not infallible. Also, clip the advertisements for the store specials you buy. They will be of great interest to you in the future. In so many words, the more you know about Alexander dolls, the more you will enjoy collecting them.

9. Restoration has made many excellent dolls near mint. Learn how to redo doll hair. Study publications that show you how to revamp textiles and fabrics. NEVER, however, practice on an expensive older doll. There are many opinions on how much, if anything, to do to "fix-up" an older doll. Listen to the options and opinions, and then decide what your personal philosophy will be. It is YOUR collection, and it should reflect your ideals and standards. This is a good time to mention that not all family members or friends will "understand" your collection. Laugh it off, and remember that you have the right to enjoy the hobby of your choice. Try to avoid the word "investment" when referring to your collection. Most likely your dolls will rise in value. If you have followed most of the suggestions above, it is a virtual certainty that fine art objects such as Madame Alexander dolls will appreciate over the years. Investments should be left to your accountant, and your doll collection should be FUN!

10. Finally, don't overlook the fellowship and friendships that doll collecting offers. The doll show circuit is filled with people just like yourself. There are Conventions devoted to Madame Alexander dolls, and ads placed by other collectors. One thing I have learned is that doll collectors seem to gravitate to each other, and lifestyles, age, and wealth, are not the barrier to relationships often seen in the outside world. This is a great hobby, filled with fascinating and intelligent individuals. DO reach out to just one collector, and I'll bet within a month, you will find more new friends than you could ever imagine!

A 14in (36cm) all composition *Margaret O'Brien*, is a collector's dream. In addition to being in mint as new condition, she has her clover leaf wrist tag with her name.

Yes, the world of doll collecting is a wonderful, fun filled place. With just a little effort, time, and education, you can learn so much. Funny, this advice sounds just like Madame Alexander, doesn't it? Her goal was not only to create beautiful dolls, but to educate her customers, and open up a world of history, art and fables. By studying, and reaching out to fellow collectors, you can obtain the goals Madame Alexander strived to achieve. Why not make your collection reflect the very best that life has to offer. Doll collecting, and especially Madame Alexander dolls, can not only be fun, but educational as well for all of us at any point in time.

A collection of Madame Alexander dolls makes life just a little more fun. Get involved today!

Alexander Doll Faces

The Alexander Doll Company has produced thousands of dolls, over a span of seventy years! Known as a fashion designer, and not a doll artist, Madame Alexander created most of her often award winning characters out of just a few basic doll faces. Some characters, especially celebrities like *Jane Withers, Sonja Henie,* and *Shari Lewis,* had a unique head designed for the company. Most of the never-ending parade of art and literary figures, storybook and nursery rhyme characters, and beloved dolls of royalty and film stars, were brought to life with the skilled use of a combination of clothing design, hairstyles, and make-up. It is a cherished tradition that continues today.

Here in our photo gallery are some famous faces that have been used for three quarters of a century. Look carefully at that face, for while featured here, the next time you see it, that face may belong to a Prince, a Queen, a fairy tale character, or even your favorite movie star!

It is not often important to identify an undressed Alexander doll. Frankly, as Madame would often say, "My figures, (dolls), are merely the mannequins upon which I drape my dreams."

Clothing labels, wrist tags, (which are often dated), and research will tell more of a doll's history than a face alone.

Some generalizations apply, with exceptions. Cloth dolls were unmarked, but jointed at the neck, and used from the 1920s into the 1930s. Composition dolls, (a mixture of sawdust, and glue, and then painted), were the mainstay of doll making until the late 1940s. Hard plastic, especially on a larger doll, generally dates the doll from the 1950s. Soft vinyl plastic on a larger doll, usually means the doll is more contemporary. One notable exception is the 8in (20cm) all hard plastic doll. Introduced as *Wendy Ann* in 1953, it still is being made today.

As with many doll companies, the date incised on the doll is the year the mold was made, and not the particular date of the character that utilized that mold. As many as three decades can pass, and a date will remain the same if that mold is still being used. As stated before, costuming and hairstyling are essential to identifying an Alexander doll.

The author would recommend the following grading system when buying, selling, or insuring your dolls.

MINT...a VERY overused term. In actuality, about 5% of dolls advertised or shown for sale fit the definition of this word. A mint doll should look like it did when it left the factory,

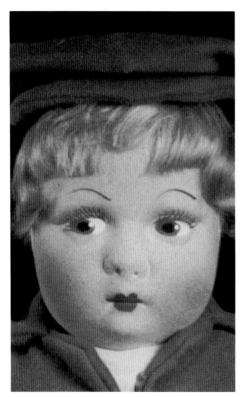

The pressed cloth face shown here was the first doll face used by the Alexander Doll Company in the 1920s and into the early 1930s. Unmarked, it has a swivel neck. Most were hand painted by Madame and her sisters!

whether 70 minutes ago, or 70 years ago! That "crisp" feeling to the clothing should be there. Facial coloring would be bright, and fresh. The wig or rooted hairstyle must be undisturbed. This type of doll is not seen as often as one would expect with the overuse of this term. Naturally, an original box, (a blessing to some collectors, and a burden to others), would add more value, as would a catalog, wrist tag, hat box, or any other accessory sold with the doll.

EXCELLENT...About 20% of dolls seen today, barring new releases are in this condition. To some, MINT and EXCELLENT are the same. To the advanced collector they are not. These terms also do NOT apply to a doll with "replaced" anything. Avoid using the phrase, "excellent, but." They can't coexist! Your excellent dolls would have everything all original, but perhaps lack that extra sparkle and crispness that a never handled doll has.

GOOD...There is certainly nothing wrong with a doll in good condition. In my opinion, the bulk of dolls found today should be graded using this word. The term, "good," as it applies to food, is certainly not a negative, and with an Alexander doll it should not be either. A constant source of conflict between buyer and seller is that the term "mint" has been used to describe a doll that is really in "good" condition. The collector of "mint" dolls generally is not looking for "good" condition dolls, even for a fair price. They would prefer a "mint" doll and should be willing to pay for it. Likewise, many collectors of "good" condition dolls do not want the expense and responsibility of a "mint" doll

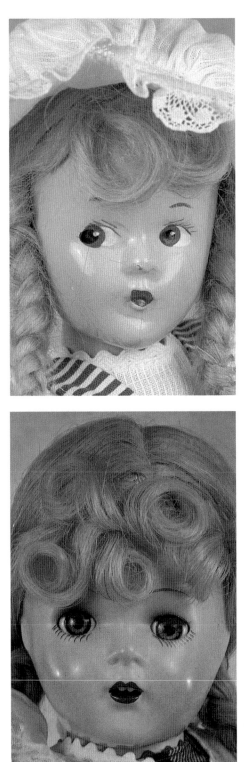

Top: This 7in (18cm) face was used on *McGuffey Ana*, as shown here, *Tiny Betty, Princess Elizabeth*, and dozens of dolls in a 7in (18cm) or 9in (23cm) size. For small dolls, it was the face used during the 1930s. The head is usually unmarked, but the body carries the Alexander name.

Bottom: A stunning *McGuffey Ana* shows yet another face used in the late 1930s and is usually marked with the "Princess Elizabeth" and Alexander name. This head mold was primarily used in the late 1930s and early 1940s on larger size dolls.

which must be carefully handled in order to keep its grading at "mint."

A "good" condition doll would have original clothing, shoes, and maybe just need some surface cleaning. To be in good condition, an Alexander doll should not have badly laundered or replaced clothing, cut hair, or missing important accessories. In reality, "good" dolls are quite desirable to many collectors.

Those who sell dolls would fair far better if prices and condition matched each other. Once again, educating people that an intelligent grading system can work is the key.

FAIR...While many Alexander dolls are bought to be "shelf dolls" or just brought out on special occasions, many, many dolls were loved and cherished by countless children. Many collectors LOVE "fair" condition dolls, AND the low prices that they SHOULD have. At the very least, one half of the listed value is subtracted for a doll in "fair" condition. Once a stigma in collecting, skilled collectors often are quite thrilled to find a pre-loved doll and restore it to as close to mint condition as possible. The skill level of this group of collectors is astonishing! Dolls that would be overlooked once, are getting a new lease on life, and making a new owner proud! This classification, in my opinion, is the one that causes the most pricing problems. A used child's toy is NOT a coveted, mint condition art object, and should be priced as such. Unless very rare, it would be hard to justify a price of much over $300 for a doll in pre-loved condition. As stated, don't

---

Top: Known for captivating collectors, this delicate face came wigged and with painted hair. It was used for 12in (31cm) versions of *Wendy-Ann*, *Alice in Wonderland*, and a few other rare characters. The body has a swivel waist, and posed hands. Usually marked, the Alexander name is most often found on the doll.

Bottom: Sonja Henie was the wealthiest woman in the world in the 1930s. In order to secure the rights to manufacture a *Sonja Henie* doll, Madame had to present a special mold. This mold was used for the *Sonja Henie* dolls, some World War II military dolls and a bride doll. It bears the name of the skating star.

overpay, whether for yourself or for resale, for many collectors would rather settle for no example of a doll, than take a less than mint doll at any price. Once you have mastered this concept, you are on your way to a successful hobby or business. I have found that doll collectors are a special breed of people, and most are more than willing to share their knowledge!

POOR... This is an often overlooked category, that affords the collector a great opportunity. Actually some dolls that are labeled in poor condition might have a fantastic wig, or original shoes. This type of doll is usually bought for "parts" for a "good" or "fair" condition doll. If you are interested in "good," or "fair" condition dolls, don't overlook a doll graded as "poor." It just might have the missing accessory you have been searching for!

As you can see, grading an Alexander doll is really quite simple as long as you remain knowledgeable about a few facts!

1. You can never make a doll "mint." It can be skillfully restored to excellent condition, but the very term, "mint" implies seamless perfection. Do not decide to collect only "mint" dolls unless you are willing to pay top prices for the very best examples. The term "mint-reasonable" has no place in a doll wanted ad!

2. Learn all you can about the "tricks of the trade." Techniques such as using boiling water to restore hair sets, and laundry methods that are state of the art, can give you a VERY fine collection at an attractive price!

Top: Margaret O'Brien was the child star of the new decade, the 1940s. Her likeness, usually marked ALEX on the head, was used in both composition and hard plastic from the 1940s into the early 1950s. It was a face that launched a thousand ships!

Bottom: Virtually the same face, only in a larger size and in the new hard plastic, this face mold first used on the *Margaret O'Brien* dolls would become the standard of beauty for the Alexander Doll Company.

3. Do realize that "good" condition dolls are NOT the step-children of collecting. Just as some collectors want only mint dolls, others are turned off by dolls they feel they can never undress, handle, or display. It is your choice, and there is no right or wrong in a hobby.

4. Do try to convince anyone who will listen that pricing an Alexander doll is just like pricing a comic book or other collectible. The condition is everything. Certainly never pay a near mint price for a played with doll.

5. While all price guides say that a guide is just that, do remember that many, many variables influence the price of a doll. Prices vary greatly throughout the country. A major doll convention in a particular area can also affect pricing. Special dolls vary greatly in price, as the good time associated with the event sometimes gets added to the price. Remember that it is your money, your hobby, and your life! Learn all you can about everything, network with other collectors, and I'll bet you will wind up with an outstanding collection, no matter what your taste and level of collecting may be.

Today is an exciting time for the collector of Madame Alexander dolls. There are all types of dolls, new and old, for just about any taste or budget. There are mint as new dolls, some real "handyman's specials." Doll shows and events that feature Madame Alexander dolls occur just about every weekend! It's a

Top: Often unmarked, but unmistakable, this full cheeked face was used in hard plastic in the early 1950s for *Kate Smith's Annabelle, Maggie Teenager, Peter Pan, Little Women, Little Men,* and many others such as brides and bridesmaids. Most of the larger size dolls used either this face or the mold first used on *Margaret O'Brien.*

Bottom: *Cissy* was Madame Alexander's entry into the world of high fashion. This face, which usually bears the Alexander Company markings, was used on child dolls such as *Binnie* and *Winnie Walker* and some of the early 1960s portrait dolls. *Cissy* was a powerful presence in the Alexander line-up.

doll's life out there! Why not get started today? With the popularity of Madame Alexander dolls, should your path change, and you wake up one day, and think WHY are all my dolls blonde, or brides, or whatever, you can sell your dolls to eager collectors and go off in another direction. Doll collecting is one of the few areas of your life today where you are in total control! That's what makes it so much fun to "children" of all ages! In my experience, the friendships made while collecting dolls are long lasting and solid. There is a whole world of interesting people, places, and dolls to see!

Note: In future editions, different faces will be highlighted, in order to complete your Alexander gallery of famous stars! To most collectors, the costume is the character, a proud tradition which continues today.

Top: Often described as coy and cute, this vinyl face was used on several girl dolls of the late 1950s, such as *Marybel, the Doll Who Gets Well, Country Cousins, Kelly* and *Pollyanna*. She bears the Alexander marking on her head.

Bottom: An impish grin in hard plastic, 8in (20cm) style, is *Maggie Mix-up* made in 1960-61. While unmarked, this head is once again a collector favorite in the 1990s. Her smile was used on angels, devils and other assorted characters of fame and fable! The body has the Alexander Doll Company name.

Top left: Another famous face is this mold that was originally used in 1957 on *Cissette*, a 10in (25cm) full figured doll, and then with heavy make-up for this *Jacqueline*. Friends *Margot*, *Gold Rush*, *Klondike Kate* and other worldly women were created from these enchanting molds. Still a popular favorite, this perky lady is the face used on the *Portrette Series*, both in the 1960s as well as the current line. The body bears the Alexander Company markings.

Top right: Always a classic in hard plastic, this *McGuffey Ana* uses the face that collectors now call *Classic Lissy*, meaning that the name *Lissy* was the most often nomenclature attached to this pursed lip pretty! Her face today makes *Hans* and *Gretl Brinker* quite a pair, and in the 1960s, she was everything from *Scarlett O'Hara* in a 12in (31cm) size, to demure little girls. This head is unmarked but with a marked Alexander body.

Left: Often called "The Face," this 8in (20cm) darling is the masthead of the Alexander Star Fleet! Originally used in 1953, this face, in one form or another, is still the *Wendy* that loves being loved! The head is unmarked, but the body bears the Alexander Company name.

Top left: Introduced as a versatile young lady in 12in (31cm) vinyl in the late 1960s, this face was utilized on the hard plastic body still in use today. From *Nancy Drew*, teen detective, to *Little Women*, this is indeed a famous visage! What other face could be BOTH *Scarlett* and *Rhett*, *Napoleon* and *Josephine*, *Antony* and *Cleopatra*, AND *Lord Fauntleroy*! Marked with the Alexander Company markings on the neck, this face was another classic like the face used on the 8in (20cm) in dolls. These faces were very versatile and chameleon like in character creation.

Top right: One of a long line of famous faces, this vinyl little girl first appeared in the mid 1960s and is still being used today. Always a 14in (36cm) size, she carries the Alexander Company markings on her neck. From *First Lady* to *McGuffey Ana*, *Alice* to *Little Orphant Annie*, this face is another Alexander doll star!

Right: The 21in (53cm) Portrait dolls, started in the 1960s, are the frosting on the cake for most collectors who would want more were it not for their imposing size. Marked on the back of the neck with the Alexander Company name, this doll was once *Jacqueline* of Camelot days, *Marie Antoinette*, and enough classic characters to fill the finest of art galleries!

Alexander Doll Designers

Daun Fallon

Growing up in California in the early 60s Daun Fallon was a true consumer of the new wave of fashion play dolls. In a world of *Barbie®*, Trolls and Little Kiddles there were three hard plastic treasures that she recalls fondly — her sisters' *Scotland* and *Mary Mary* and her very own 8in (20cm) *Ballerina*, a special doll with an intriguing detail of pink sequins that was probably responsible for Daun's career choice as a Costume Designer. She attended the University of California and after receiving a BA in Theatrical Costume Design, began a busy career as a free-lance draper. Numerous regional opera, ballet and theater companies benefited from Daun's talents. In 1988 Fallon took the plunge and came to New York City where she worked in several costume houses creating stunning costumes for Broadway smashes including *Phantom of the Opera*, *Jerome Robbins Broadway*, *Aspects of Love*, and numerous ballet companies.

Daun brings with her a vast quality of talent and imagination. Add to that a vivid memory of a *Wendy* doll in pink sequins and it isn't hard to see where award-nominated dolls such as *Tinkerbell*, *The Goldfish*, *The Scarlet Series* and all of our friends from Oz have emerged.

Therese J. Stadelmeier

Growing up in Bucks County, Pennsylvania, Therese Stadelmeier always had a passion for dolls, owning her first Alexander at the age of four and playing with them as well as her *Barbies®*. It was only shortly after that, that she became a doll designer by creating an Abigail Adams costume (1776) for her *Barbie*. But the Alexander Doll Co. had to wait for her to finish her college education. She received a BFA in Design for Theater from Penn State University and began a ten year stint creating costumes for many Broadway shows in New York (such as *Starlight Express*, *Phantom of the Opera*, *Aspects of Love*, *Cats*, *Legs Diamond*, *Will Rogers Follies*, and Sigfried and Roy in Las Vegas) before becoming a designer for the company in 1991. Extremely modest about her work, describing it as "getting to live out every little girl's fantasy," Therese has been the proud designer of such Alexander successes as the *Anne* and *Wendy Loves...* series among many others, several of which have received DOTY® and Award of Excellence nominations.

19

Preserving Your Alexander Dolls

Collectors of Alexander dolls have often been referred to as "perfectionists." In many cases this is true. The collector who has chosen to pay the price for mint in box dolls, must, by definition, be somewhat of a perfectionist. AND, it would be necessary for that collector to keep on being that way to maintain the "mint" grading of their dolls.

All this might sound pretty intimidating to the novice collector, or the casual reader of this book, but it IS possible to maintain any Alexander doll collection at the purchase level with just some good advice and plain common sense.

My own Alexander collection is made up of a few perfect mint in box dolls, that I must admit, intimidate me a bit. We have been taught that the word "investment" implies perfection, and really only some of the time that is true.

A couple of years ago, the Alexander Doll Company began a series of dolls that were eight inches tall, and dressed as angels. Casually titled, *Tree Toppers*, they were perfection itself. Speigel's has had exclusives, and the Alexander Doll Company has issued some on its own.

When I got my first doll from Spiegel's, the sheer wonder of that perfect little angelic tree topper in the box was awesome! It took we a week to get up the nerve to just remove the neck brace, which was stapled to the sides of the box. (If you don't understand any of this, then you are truly a new collector or a casual observer.)

Finally, when I removed that incredible creature, and put her where she belonged, on top of my Christmas tree, I felt like a recovering "never take it from the box" collector! The happiness that doll brought to me, my family, my neighbors, and friends, would fill this book. My friends noticed my

OTHER dolls, and even my family was spellbound by the majesty that this Tree Topper dealt from her lofty place!

After the holidays, I carefully returned my little angel to her box, and lo and behold, guess what! She had not suffered a bit! Her gown was still radiant; her halo angelic, and her pursed lips were still serene! I had broken the spell of the boxed doll! She had survived, and so did I!

The moral of this story is that even the highest quality mint in box Alexander doll CAN be enjoyed out of its box AND not suffer in the hands of a skilled collector. One has to remember that one does own their doll collection and not the other way around!

One of the nicer things about Alexander dolls, for the most part, is that they are not shrink wrapped and sealed in boxes. Unlike some other dolls, notably fashion dolls, they can be removed from their boxes, observed, photographed, gently handled, and still not lose their "mint" grading. They are not held prisoner by cellophane and cardboard, but float loose in the box, to be set free by the new owner.

In one of my early encounters with Madame Alexander at a doll show in New England in the late 1970s, I asked Madame why her doll boxes did not portray the gorgeous artwork that fashion dolls, character dolls, and celebrity dolls did? Smiling, Madame said that the box was, and I quote, "merely the shipping carton for the doll to arrive safely from us to you. We are creating dolls, NOT boxes!" Well, I guess I knew from then on that an Alexander box is not the shrine that some collectors make it out to be!

How then can the collector who is buying a "mint" graded doll enjoy it without

Rarely does one find a composition Alexander doll is such incredible condition. This 1930s vintage *McGuffey Ana* is all original, complete with her "schoolhouse" wrist tag. She did not come with a hat as shown on her wrist tag. Keeping her in excellent condition involves common sense as outlined in this chapter!

Simple Rules to Preserve Alexander Dolls

1 If you do buy a mint in box Alexander doll, whether old or new, replace the tissue paper with acid free tissue. This can be found at art supply houses, craft stores, and even dry cleaners that specialize in wedding gown cleaning. This will prevent the acid in the tissue and cardboard from reacting with the fabric and the doll. Surprised? Yes, the box is NOT often the best place for your doll to be kept! If the original tissue captivates you, put it in a baggie and keep it in the box.

2 Sunlight, even normal room light is a real enemy of dolls. Fabrics fade gradually. Sometimes it isn't until you take a doll out of a cabinet years later do you notice that the sun has faded the front of the doll's outfit. This does NOT mean that you can never have a doll on display in a "normal" room. Just be sure that direct sunlight does not hit the doll, and rotate the dolls in the room from time to time. Seasonal displays are one reason to collect dolls. Don't deny yourself the pleasure of a holiday display out of fear of harming your doll. Common sense is the password.

3 Children, pets, and dolls do not mix. They can, but keep the dolls high, and the rest low! Seriously, your five year old can't tell that your "Cissy" is over thirty years old. You can also be sure that the plastic still smells mighty good to your "man's best friend," so prevention is the key. Don't mix the deadly triangle of pets, plastic, and pretty children!

4 As mentioned above, enjoy your dolls. Why have them, if they are just listed in a notebook, and stuffed in a closet? (Sometimes, they don't even make a notebook!) Great that you went to Disney World® and stayed up all night to get that Alexander exclusive! Now what! Put the precious thing under a dome, or in a display, and love it to death! That IS why you bought it, isn't it!

5 Despite what some well meaning curators, and gloom and doom "experts" say, sensible handling and displaying of your dolls will NOT make them lose a grade. For the collector of "good" condition dolls, this may be a chapter they think they can skip over. NOT SO! Any doll, if exposed to sunlight, insects, pets, extremes in temperature, and ill handling, (from the very young on up), CAN suffer greatly. I often think of a doll as a wonderful piece of jewelry. It enhances the owner's beauty, when worn and displayed, but does nothing in a safety deposit box except tarnish! It's the same with dolls!

destroying it? Easy! There are just a few, simple rules!

Finally, don't you think that it's time we started ENJOYING our dolls more? I give programs all over the United States, and I love photographing my own dolls, the dolls that come through my business, and my friends' dolls. Fun times are shared as we laugh and turn a little head just to capture a twinkle in an eye, or the sheen of a taffeta dress. Never once in fifteen years, has a doll suffered during a photo shoot. If anything, I examined the doll more closely before the

photo, and tamed a stray hair, or fluffed up a dress. Like us, dolls seem to thrive on love and attention.

I guess the above mentioned topics will ruffle some feathers from the "don't touch" crowd, but as I stated, none of my dolls have ever suffered from careful display and handling, while I have had clothing disintegrate from acids in the box! The bottom line is, enjoy your dolls, and I think your doll collecting will be whole lot more fun! I sure think so, and I'll bet you will too!

Madame Alexander Doll Values

Many, many generous collectors and dealers helped with the formulation of the listings and prices. Besides those credited, there are over a dozen collectors who wish to remain anonymous, and their help is greatly appreciated.

In some other sources of information about Madame Alexander dolls, and the Alexander Doll Company, you may notice additional dolls listed and substantial value discrepancies.

I have made every attempt not to include a doll unless I personally had either seen the doll or a photograph of the same. The next step was to ask if the doll is documented by either a clothing label stating the name of the character, a wrist tag stating the same, or an original box with a character name. Catalogs, not only from the Alexander Doll Company but from many well-known department stores and mail order firms, were examined. I welcome your ideas with documented proof that additional Alexander dolls exist. My goal is to author "The Definitive Identification and Value Guide on Alexander Dolls."

Knowing that this may be a challenge, I want to be satisfied that every research material has been examined before being listed.

Finally, some collectors are interested in the dolls dressed by the designers of the Ice Capades. These dolls and values were not included because, in my opinion, they were not dressed in clothing designed at the Alexander Doll Company factory, and while very collectible, I do not feel they should be included in a book about clothing design from a specific company.

My goal here is not to dictate, not to pronounce judgment on any collection, but to offer a quality and as error free product as humanly possible to enhance the enjoyment of our collections.

Values are a touchy subject. They are necessary to insure our collections, substantiate a loss, and create a starting point in our dealings with each other.

A guide is just that, a guide. Ultimately only you, the buyer, can determine the "right" price. My goal is to try to assist the novice, and help the dedicated, in their pursuit of Alexander Doll Company treasures.

Information is the key to enjoying any hobby. Many have shared that information with me in compiling these listings and prices. Research material is welcomed, so that we can all better our collections through education.

We, as collectors of Alexander Doll Company dolls, are most fortunate. As a collecting body, we still have many beautiful and perfect examples of the lovely creations designed by Madame Alexander herself. We also are benefiting from the extraordinary contributions of the Alexander Doll Company design team today, who have the respect for tradition and the foresight to expand into new and innovative concepts.

One thing we can be sure of is that quality, desirability, and enjoyment potential is in each and every Alexander Doll Company product. The new motto of the Alexander Doll Company is, "It's a Madame Alexander, say no more."

Alexander Dolls are an American tradition that bring a sense of continuity to our lives. Let's make our hobby the best that it can be, and unite the past and the present to make, as Madame Alexander often stated, a thing of beauty, a joy, forever...

ABBREVIATIONS

MADC - Madame Alexander Doll Club
LE - Limited Edition
FAD - Factory Altered Doll
EDH - Enchanted Doll House
CU - Collector's United

UFDC - United Federation of Doll Clubs
NECS - New England Collector's Society
S/A - Still Available
N/A - Information not available

NOTE: Prices are based on excellent to mint dolls.

A **ACTIVE MISS** 18" (46cm) hard plastic, 1954 ....$ 875.00
ADAMS, ABIGAIL 1st set, First Ladies Series, 1976-1978 ....100.00
ADAMS, LOUISA 1st set, First Ladies Series, 1976-1978 ....100.00
AFRICA 8" (20cm) hard plastic, bend knee, 1966-1971 ....250.00
   8" (20cm) hard plastic, straight leg, re-issued 1988-1992 ....52.00
AGATHA 8" (20cm) hard plastic, black top and floral gown,
   1953-1954 ....950.00
   18" (46cm) hard plastic, pink taffeta, Me and My
      Shadow Series, 1954 ....1500.00
   21" (53cm) Portrait, red gown, 1967 ....525.00
   10" (25cm) Portrette, red velvet, 1968..395.00
   21" (53cm) Portrait, rose gown with cape, 1974 ....350.00
   21" (53cm) Portrait, blue with white sequin trim, 1975 ....250.00
   21" (53cm) Portrait, blue with white rick-rack trim, 1976 ....250.00
   21" (53cm) Portrait, lavender, 1979-1980 ....200.00
   21" (53cm) Portrait, turquoise, 1981 ....200.00
AGNES cloth, 1930s 750.00
ALADDIN 8" (20cm), Storyland Dolls, 1993 ....50.00
ALASKA 8" (20cm), Americana Series, 1990-1991 ....50.00

The early cloth dolls in the 1920s were hand painted by Madame Alexander and her sisters. This Dicken's character was part of a series.

ALBANIA   8" (20cm) straight leg, 1987 .... $ 80.00
ALCOTT, LOUISA MAY   14" (36cm), 1989-1990 .... 80.00
   8" (20cm) hard plastic, Storyland Dolls, 1992 .... 55.00
Alexander Rag Time Dolls   cloth, 1938-1939 .... 900.00
ALEXANDER-KINS   7½-8" (19-20cm) hard plastic (sometimes called
   Wendy, Wendy-Ann or Wendy-kins).
   Straight leg non-walker, 1953.
      Coat, hat (dress) 450.00
      Cotton dress, organdy pinafore, hat 450.00
      Cotton dress, cotton pinafore, hat 450.00
      Day in Country long gown 650.00-750.00
      Easter doll (early version) .... 1000.00 up
      Felt jackets, pleated dresses 550.00
      Garden Party gown 650.00
      Jumper, bodysuit 325.00
      Nightgown 325.00
      Nude, perfect doll 300.00
      Organdy dress, pinafore, hat 350.00
      Robe or P.J.s 175.00
      Satin dress, pinafore, hat 375.00
      Sleeveless pinafore 325.00
      Taffeta dress, cotton pinafore, hat 395.00
   Straight leg walker, 1955.
      Basic doll in box, panties, shoes, socks 375.00
      Coat, hat 350.00

This cloth *Dionne Quintuplet* doll is considered a classic with collectors. Just imagine having all five in this mint condition.

Cotton dress, pinafore, hat ....$ 350.00
Cotton school dress 250.00
Day in the Country 650.00
Garden Party long gown 550.00
Maypole Dance 650.00
Nightgown 150.00
Nude, perfect doll 275.00
Organdy dress, hat 350.00
P.J.s 145.00
Riding habit 275.00
Robe, P.J.s 145.00
Sailor dress 500.00
Sleeveless organdy dress 250.00
Swimsuits 225.00
Taffeta party dress/hat 375.00
Bend knee walker, 1956-1964.
Basic doll in box, panties, shoes, socks 275.00
Carcoat 375.00
Cherry Twin .... 900.00 up
Coat, hat (dress) 275.00
Cotton dress, pinafore/hat 300.00
Cotton or satin dress, pinafore/hat 300.00
Felt jacket/pleated skirt/dress/hat 400.00
First dancing dress 450.00
Flowergirl .... 750.00 up

Alexander Doll Company press release photo showing actress Rochelle Hudson admiring genuine *Dionne Quintuplet* dolls. *Alexander Doll Company, Bob Gantz, photographer.*

June Wedding .... $ 550.00
Long party dress 650.00
Neiman Marcus doll in case, all clothes .... 1000.00 up
Nightgown, robe 200.00
Nude 175.00
Organdy dress, organdy pinafore/hat 375.00
Riding habit, boy 375.00
Riding habit, corduroy, girl 375.00
Skater 250.00
Sleeveless school dress 250.00
Sundress 250.00
Swimsuits, beach outfits 250.00
Taffeta dress, hat 350.00
Velvet party dress 350.00
Bend knee, non-walkers, 1965-1972.
Basic doll with panties, shoes, socks 175.00
Cotton dress, 1965 .... 150.00
Easter doll .... 1000.00 up
Felt jacket, skirt, dress, cap, hat, 1965 .... 550.00
French braid, cotton dress, 1965 .... 550.00
Nude, perfect doll 85.00
Organdy dress, hat, 1965 .... 275.00
Riding habit, check pants, boy, 1965 .... 325.00
Riding habit, check pants, girl, 1965 .... 275.00
Sewing kit doll 1000.00

Alexander Doll Company publicity photo showing the *Dionne Quintuplet* dolls at play! Special molds were used to create these composition dolls dating from around 1936. *Alexander Doll Company, Bob Gantz, photographer.*

ALGERIA   8" (20cm) straight leg, 1988 ....$ 75.00
ALICE (SOMETIMES CALLED ALICE IN WONDERLAND)
   16" (41cm) cloth, 1930s .... 600.00 up
   7" (18cm) composition, 1930s 350.00
   9" (23cm) composition, 1930s 350.00
   11-14" (28-36cm) composition, 1936-1940 .... 450.00
   13" (33cm) composition, swivel waist, 1930s 400.00
   14½-18" (37-46cm) composition, 1948-1949 .... 500.00
   21" (53cm) composition, 1948-1949 .... 950.00
   14" (36cm) hard plastic, 1950 .... 575.00
   14½" (37cm) hard plastic, 1949-1950 .... 650.00 up
   14" (36cm) hard plastic with trousseau, 1951-1952 .... 1500.00 up
   17-23" (43-58cm) hard plastic, 1949-1950 .... 750.00
   18" (46cm) hard plastic, 1951 .... 750.00
   29" (74cm) cloth, vinyl, 1952 .... 575.00
   15" (38cm), 18" (46cm), 23" (58cm) hard plastic, 1951-1952 .... 700.00
   8" (20cm) hard plastic, 1955-1956 .... 650.00
   14" (36cm) plastic/vinyl, 1966-1992 .... 74.00
   8" (20cm) hard plastic, Disney Crest Color, (Disneyland®,
   Disney World®), 1972-1976 (*see Special Dolls*) 450.00

A 7in (18cm) piece of perfection, *McGuffey Ana* was a popular theme for dolls for over sixty years!

8" (20cm), 1990-1992 ....$ 47.00
8" (20cm), red trim, 1993...47.00
ALICE AND THE WHITE RABBIT   10" (25cm), made for Disney, 1991
(*see Special Dolls*) 325.00
ALL STAR   8" (20cm), white or black, Americana Series, 1993 ....55.00
ALLISON   18" (46cm) cloth, vinyl, 1990-1991 ....100.00
ALPINE CHRISTMAS TWINS   8" (20cm), made for Christmas Shoppe, 1992
(*see Special Dolls*) 165.00
ALTAR BOY   8" (20cm) hard plastic, Americana Series, 1991 ....45.00
AMANDA   8" (20cm) hard plastic, Americana Series, 1961 ....1200.00 up
AMERICAN BEAUTY   10" (25cm), Portrette, 1991-1992 ....80.00
AMERICAN GIRL   7-8" (18-20cm) composition, 1938 ....325.00
9-11" (23-28cm) composition, 1937 ....400.00
8" (20cm) hard plastic, 1962-1963, called "McGuffey Ana"
in 1964-1965 ....350.00
AMERICAN INDIAN   9" (23cm) composition, 1938-1939 ....300.00
AMERICAN TOTS   16-21" (41-53cm), cloth dressed in
children's fashions 450.00
AMERICAN WOMEN'S VOLUNTEER SERVICE (AWVS)   14" (36cm)
composition, 1942 ....750.00

The same 24in (61cm) *McGuffey Ana* doll from the 1930s is made of all composition and sports a human hair wig.

AMISH BOY   8" (20cm) hard plastic, bend knee, Americana Series,
1966-1969 .... $ 250.00
AMISH GIRL   8" (20cm) hard plastic, bend knee, Americana Series,
1966-1969 .... 350.00
AMY   (*see Little Women*)
ANASTASIA   10" (25cm), Portrette Series, 1988-1989 .... 75.00
ANASTASIA   14" (36cm), MADC Convention Special .... S/A
ANATOLIA   8" (20cm) straight leg, 1987-1988 .... 50.00
ANGEL   8" (20cm), in pink, blue, white gowns, 1950s .... 750.00 up
8" (20cm), Guardian, 1954 .... 750.00 up
8" (20cm), hard plastic, Baby, 1955 .... 750.00 up
ANGEL FACE   8" (20cm), made for Shirley's Doll House, 1990
(*see Special Dolls*) 125.00
ANNA BALLERINA   18" (46cm) composition, 1940 .... 750.00
ANNA KARENINA   21" (53cm), Portrait, 1991 .... 335.00
ANNABELLE   14-15" (36-38cm) hard plastic, 1951-1952 .... 500.00
14-15" (36-38cm), trousseau/trunk, 1952 .... 1500.00
18" (46cm) hard plastic, 1951-1952 .... 650.00
20-23" (51-58cm) hard plastic, 1951-1952 .... 750.00
29" (74cm) vinyl and cloth, 1952 (Barbara Jane) 600.00
8" (20cm), made for Belk & Leggett, 1992 (*see Special Dolls*) 78.00
ANNE OF GREEN GABLES
14" (36cm), Anne Goes to School, with trunk, wardrobe, 1992-1993 .... 250.00
14" (36cm), Arrives at Station, 1992-1993 .... 140.00
14" (36cm), Anne Becomes the Teacher, 1993 .... 125.00
Puff sleeve dress, 1992 .... 40.00
White organdy dress, 1992 .... 45.00
Winter coat outfit, 1992 .... 45.00

A charming little girl tells a 24in (61cm) 1930s *McGuffey Ana* doll to be quiet. (Note that no hat came with this outfit.) *Alexander Doll Company, Bob Gantz, photographer.*

ANNIE LAURIE   14" (36cm) composition, 1937 .... $ 575.00
   17" (43cm) composition, 1937 .... 875.00
ANTOINETTE   21" (53cm) composition, 1946 .... 2000.00
ANTONY, MARK   12" (31cm), Portraits of History, 1980-1985 .... 50.00
APPLE ANNIE   8" (20cm) hard plastic, 1954 .... 950.00 up
APPLE PIE   14" (36cm), Classic Dolls, 1991 .... 85.00
APRIL   14" (36cm), Classic Dolls, 1990-1991 .... 95.00
ARGENTINE BOY   8" (20cm) hard plastic, bend knee walker, 1965 .... 450.00
   8" (20cm) hard plastic, bend knee, 1965 .... 375.00
ARGENTINE GIRL   8" (20cm) bend knee walker, 1965 .... 175.00
   8" (20cm) hard plastic, bend knee, 1965-1972 .... 125.00
   8" (20cm) hard plastic, straight legs, 1973-1976 .... 60.00
   8" (20cm) hard plastic, straight legs, 1976-1986 .... 55.00
ARMENIA   8" (20cm) 1989-1990 .... 50.00
ARRIVING IN AMERICA   8" (20cm) hard plastic,
Americana Series, 1992-1993 .... 55.00
ARTIE   12" (31cm) plastic, vinyl, made for FAO Schwarz, 1962 .... 275.00
ASHLEY   8" (20cm), jacket, hat, Scarlett Series, 1990 .... 70.00
   8" (20cm) hard plastic, Confederate Officer, Scarlett Series, 1991 .... 55.00
ASTROLOGICAL DOLLS OF THE MONTH   14-17" (36-43cm) composition,
   1938 .... 450.00
AUNT AGATHA   8" (20cm) hard plastic, 1957 .... 950.00
AUNT BETSY   Cloth, felt, 1930s 850.00
AUNT PITTY PAT   14-17" (36-43cm) composition, 1939 .... 1200.00 up
   8" (20cm) hard plastic, 1957 .... 1500.00
   8" (20cm) hard plastic, straight leg, Scarlett Series, 1991-1992 .... 57.00
AUSTRALIA   8" (20cm), 1990-1991 .... 55.00
AUSTRIA BOY*   Straight legs, 1973-1975 .... 60.00
   1976-1989 .... 55.00
AUSTRIA GIRL*   Straight legs, 1973-1975 .... 60.00
   1976-1990 .... 55.00
*Formerly Tyrolean Boy and Girl
AUTUMN   14" (36cm), Classic Dolls, 1993 .... 135.00
AUTUMN IN N.Y.   10" (25cm), made for First Modern Doll Club, 1991
   (see Special Dolls) 225.00
AVRIL, JANE   10" (25cm), made for Marshall Fields, 1989,
   (see Special Dolls) 195.00

B   BABBIE   Cloth, inspired by Katherine Hepburn 1950.00
BABETTE   10" (25cm), Portrette Series, 1988-1989 .... 75.00
BABS SKATER   18" (46cm) composition 650.00
   15" (38cm) hard plastic, 1948-1950 .... 650.00
   17-18" (43-46cm) hard plastic 750.00
   21" (53cm) hard plastic .... 800.00 up
BABY BETTY   10-12" (25-31cm) composition, 1935-1936 .... 250.00
BABY BROTHER AND SISTER   20" (51cm) cloth, vinyl, 1977-1979 .... 75.00 each
   14" (36cm), 1979-1982 .... 80.00 each
   14" (36cm), re-introduced 1989 .... 60.00 each
BABY CLOWN   8" (20cm) hard plastic, painted face, 1955 .... 1200.00 up
BABY ELLEN   14" (36cm), 1965-1972 .... 100.00
BABY GENIUS   11" (28cm), all cloth, 1930s 450.00
   11-12" (28-31cm) composition, cloth, 1930s-1940s 165.00
   16" (41cm) composition, cloth, 1930s-1940s 175.00
   15" (38cm) hard plastic head, vinyl limbs, 1949-1950 .... 150.00
   18" (46cm) hard plastic head, vinyl limbs, 1949-1950 .... 250.00

21" (53cm) hard plastic head, vinyl limbs, 1949-1950 ....$ 350.00
8" (20cm) hard plastic, vinyl, 1956-1962 (*see Litte Genius*)
BABY JANE 16" (41cm) composition, 1935 .... 875.00 up
BABY LYNN 20" (51cm) cloth, vinyl, 1973-1976 .... 100.00
BABY MCGUFFEY 22-24" (56-61cm) composition, 1937 .... 300.00
20" (51cm) cloth, vinyl, 1971-1976 .... 200.00
14" (36cm) cloth, vinyl, 1972-1978 .... 150.00
BABY PRECIOUS 14" (36cm) cloth, vinyl, 1975 .... 70.00
21" (53cm) cloth, vinyl, 1974-discontinued 1976 .... 90.00
BAD LITTLE GIRL 16" (41cm) cloth, blue dress, companion to
Good Little Girl, 1966.. 90.00
BALI 8" (20cm), International Dolls, 1993 .... 50.00
BALLERINA (*also see individual dolls*)
9" (23cm) composition, 1935-1941 .... 300.00
11-14" (28-36cm) composition, 1936-1938 .... 400.00
17" (43cm) composition, 1938-1941 .... 500.00
21" (53cm) hard plastic, Deborah Ballerina, 1947 .... 3000.00
15-18" (38-46cm) hard plastic, 1950-1952 .... 550.00

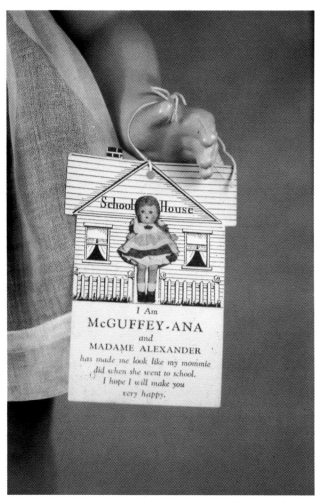

Collectors call this rare wrist tag, "The Schoolhouse," because it ties in *McGuffey Ana* to the McGuffy Readers that generations grew up with. The tag includes a photo of the outfit and proof that this outfit did not come with a hat.

8" (20cm) hard plastic straight leg non-walker, lavender,
  yellow, pink, 1953 ....$ 750.00
    blue (rare) 850.00
8" (20cm) hard plastic, straight leg walker, lavender, yellow,
  pink, blue, 1954-1955 ....500.00
    8" (20cm), white, 1955 ....550.00
    8" (20cm), rose, 1956 ....550.00
    8" (20cm), yellow, 1956 ....450.00
15" (38cm) hard plastic, Binnie, 1956 ....285.00
18" (46cm) hard plastic, Binnie, 1956 ....375.00
10" (25cm) hard plastic, 1957-1959 ....425.00
12" (31cm) hard plastic, Lissy, 1956, 1958 ....400.00
16½" (42cm), Elise Ballerina, jointed at ankle, knee, hip, elbow
  and shoulder, 1957-1964 ....350.00
    16½ (42cm) hard plastic, 1957 ....350.00
    16½ (42cm) hard plastic, white tutu, 1958 ....350.00
    16½ (42cm) hard plastic, gold tutu and slippers, 1959 ....350.00
    16 ½ (42cm) hard plastic, pink tutu, 1960 ....350.00
    16½ (42cm) hard plastic, pink tutu (upswept hairdo), 1961 ....350.00
    16½ (42cm) hard plastic, blue tutu, 1962 ....350.00

16in (41cm) all-composi-
tion *McGuffey Ana* is mint-
in-box in her complete outfit with octagon shaped
wrist tag. Dolls this mint
often bring much more than
list price.

16½ (42cm), blue tutu, variation of face and hair piece: wreath
   of small flowers (1963), large flowers (1964), 1963-1964 .... $ 350.00
8" (20cm), bend knee walker, 1957-1965 .... 450.00
   8" (20cm), blue, 1957 .... 400.00
   8" (20cm), pink, 1958 .... 350.00
   8" (20cm), gold, 1959 .... 450.00
   8" (20cm), lavender, 1961 .... 550.00
8" (20cm), bend knee, yellow, 1965-1972 .... 375.00
   8" (20cm), blue, 1962-1972 .... 225.00
   8" (20cm), pink, 1962-1972 .... 200.00
14" (36cm), 1965 .... 375.00
17" (43cm) plastic, vinyl, discontinued costume, 1967-1989 .... 95.00
17" (43cm), 1970-1971 .... 325.00
14" (36cm) plastic, vinyl, 1973-1982 .... 165.00
8" (20cm) straight leg, 1973-1992 (1985-1987 white face) 60.00
8" (20cm), ballerina trunk set, made for Enchanted Doll House, 1983
   (see Special Dolls) 185.00
8" (20cm), Ballerina, MADC, 1984 (see Special Dolls) 250.00
8" (20cm), made for Enchanted Doll House, 1989 (see Special Dolls) 95.00
12" (31cm), Muffin, 1989-1990 .... 70.00
12" (31cm), Romance Collection, 1990-1992 .... 72.00
8" (20cm), white/gold, Americana Series, 1990-1993,
   black or white dolls, 1991 .... 65.00
   pink, black or white doll, 1992 .... 52.00

The Little Colonel dolls, based on the best selling book, made a great display in the Alexander Doll Company's New York showroom in the late 1930s. Today these dolls are very hard to find and are highly prized by collectors. *Alexander Doll Company, Bob Gantz, photographer.*

17" (43cm) plastic, vinyl, "Firebird" and "Swan Lake," 1990-1991 .... $ 125.00
12" (31cm), Ballerina, 1993 (Classic Lissy) 95.00
21" (53cm) vinyl, Lilac Fairie Ballerina, 1993 (vinyl Cissy) 300.00
BARBARA JANE   29" (74cm) cloth, vinyl, 1952 .... 400.00
BARBARY COAST   10" (25cm) hard plastic, Portrette Series, 1962-1963 .... 1200.00
BARTON, CLARA   10" (25cm), Portrette Series, 1989 .... 75.00
BATHING BEAUTY   10" (25cm), UFDC Special Doll, 1992
(see Special Dolls) 300.00
BEAST   12" (31cm), Romance Series, 1992 .... 115.00
BEAUX ART DOLLS   18" (46cm) hard plastic, 1953 .... 1500.00
BEAU BRUMMEL   Cloth, 1930s 725.00
BEAUTY   12" (31cm), Romance Series, 1992 .... 105.00
BEAUTY QUEEN   10" (25cm) hard plastic, 1961 (see Cissette) 225.00
BEDDY-BYE BROOKE   14" (36cm), made for FAO Schwarz, 1991
(see Special Dolls) 90.00
BEDDY-BYE BROOKE & BRENDA   14" (36cm) and 8" (20cm), made for
FAO Schwarz, 1992 (see Special Dolls) 175.00
BELLE OF THE BALL   10" (25cm), Portrette Series, 1989 .... 65.00
BELGIUM   7" (18cm) composition, 1935-1938 .... 325.00
8" (20cm) hard plastic, bend knee, 1972 .... 100.00
8" (20cm) straight legs, 1973-1975 .... 60.00
8" (20cm) straight legs, 1976-1988 .... 55.00
BELLE WATLING   10" (25cm), Scarlett Series, 1992 .... 90.00
BELLOWS' ANNE   14" (36cm) plastic, vinyl, Fine Arts Series, 1987 .... 75.00
BERNHARDT, SARAH   21" (53cm), dressed in all burgundy, 1987 .... 250.00

Alexander Doll Company publicity photo shows *The Dicken's Collection* from the early 1930s.
Alexander Doll Company, Bob Gantz, photographer.

BESSY BELL   14" (36cm) plastic, vinyl, Classic Dolls, 1988 .... $ 70.00
BESSY BROOKS   8" (20cm), Storyland Dolls, 1988-1991 .... 55.00
BESSY BROOKS BRIDE   8" (20cm), Greenville Show, 1990
    (*see Special Dolls*) 100.00
BEST MAN   8" (20cm) hard plastic, 1955 .... 650.00
BETH   (*see Little Women*)
BETH   10" (25cm), made for Spiegel, 1990 (*see Special Dolls*) 150.00
BETTY   12" (31cm) composition, 1936-1937 .... 400.00
    14" (36cm) composition, 1935-1942 .... 325.00
    16-18" (41-46cm) composition, 1935-1942 .... 375.00
    19-21" (48-53cm) composition, 1938-1941 .... 375.00
    14½-17½ (37-45cm) hard plastic, made for Sears in 1951 .... 485.00
    30" (76cm) plastic, vinyl, 1960 .... 385.00
BETTY, LITTLE   9" (23cm) composition, 1935-1943 .... 295.00
BETTY, TINY   7" (18cm) composition, 1934-1943 .... 325.00
BETTY BAG   All cloth, flat painted face, yarn hair, 1940s 300.00
BETTY BLUE   8" (20cm) straight leg, Storyland Dolls, 1987-1988 only 60.00
BIBLE CHARACTER DOLLS   8" (20cm) hard plastic, 1954 .... 6000.00
BILL   8" (20cm) hard plastic, 1955-1963 .... 550.00
    Groom, 1953-1957 .... 525.00
BINNIE WALKER   15-18" (38-46cm) hard plastic, 1954-1955 .... 125.00-250.00
    15" (38cm) in trunks, wardrobe 950.00
    15" (38cm) Skater, hard plastic, 1955 .... 600.00

1939 was a big year for Oscar winning movies. This publicity still of *Walt Disney's® Snow White* dolls was taken in the New York City showroom. A collector's dream come true. *Alexander Doll Company, Bob Gantz, photographer.*

18" (46cm) Toddler, plastic, vinyl, 1964 ....$ 325.00 up
25" (64cm) hard plastic, 1954-1955 ....450.00
25" (64cm) in formals, 1955 ....475.00 up
BIRTHDAY, HAPPY   MADC, 1985 (*see Special Dolls*) 365.00
BIRTHDAY DOLLS   7" (18cm) composition 325.00
BITSEY   11-12" (28-31cm) composition, 1942-1946 ....225.00
11-16" (28-41cm), head hard plastic, 1949-1951 ....150.00
12" (31cm) cloth, vinyl, 1965-1966 ....125.00
19-26" (48-66cm), 1949-1951 ....150.00-200.00
BITSEY, LITTLE   9" (23cm) all vinyl, 1967-1968 ....95.00
11-16" (28-41cm) 30.00-175.00
BLACK FOREST   8" (20cm), 1989-1991 ....60.00
BLISS, BETTY TAYLOR   2nd set, First Ladies Series, 1979-1981 ....105.00
Blue Boy   7" (18cm) composition, 1936-1938 ....325.00
9" (23cm) composition, 1938-1941 ....350.00
12" (31cm) plastic, vinyl, Portrait Children, 1972-1983 ....70.00
In blue velvet, 1985-1987 ....95.00
BLUE DANUBE WALTZ
18" (46cm) hard plastic, blue taffeta, Me and My Shadow Series, 1954 ..1200.00 up
BLUE FAIRIE   10" (25cm), Portrette Series, 1993 ....85.00

A gorgeous, mint 1930s all-composition *Sonja Henie* doll with a mohair wig. (Some deluxe models had human hair.)

BLUE MOON   14" (36cm), Classic Dolls, 1991-1992 ....$ 170.00
BLUE ZIRCON   10" (25cm), Birthday Collection, 1992 ....64.00
BO PEEP, LITTLE   7" (18cm) composition, Storyland Dolls, 1937-1941 ....325.00
  9-11" (23-28cm) composition, 1936-1940..325.00
  7½" (19cm) hard plastic, straight leg walker, 1955 ....450.00
  8" (20cm) hard plastic, bend knee walker, 1962-1964 ....375.00
  8" (20cm) hard plastic, bend knee, 1965-1972 ....135.00
  8" (20cm) hard plastic, straight leg, 1973-1975...60.00
  8" (20cm) hard plastic, 1976-1986 ....55.00
  14" (36cm), Classic Dolls, 1988-1989 ....60.00
  12" (31cm) porcelain, 1990-1992 ....255.00
  14" (36cm), re-introduced 1992-1993 ....132.00
BOBBIE SOX   8" (20cm) hard plastic, made for Disney, 1990
  (*see Special Dolls*) 150.00
BOBBY   8" (20cm) hard plastic, 1957 ....465.00
  8" (20cm) hard plastic, 1960 ....500.00
BOBBY Q.   Cloth, 1940-1942 ....625.00 up
BOBO CLOWN   8" (20cm), 1991-1992 ....52.00
BOHEMIA   8" (20cm), 1989-1991 ....50.00
BOLIVIA   8" (20cm) hard plastic, bend knee and bend knee walker,
  1963-1966 ....250.00 up
BON VOYAGE LITTLE MISS MAGNIN   8" (20cm), made for I. Magnin,
  1993 (*see Special Dolls*) ....S/A
BON VOYAGE MISS MAGNIN   10" (25cm), made for I. Magnin, 1993
  (*see Special Dolls*) ....S/A

Publicity still showing many variations of *Sonja Henie* dolls available in the late 1930s. What a collector's delight! *Alexander Doll Company, Bob Gantz, photographer.*

BONNIE (BABY) 16-19" (41-48cm) vinyl, 1954-1955 .... $ 80.00
    24-30" (61-76cm), 1954-1955 .... 165.00
BONNIE BLUE #1305, 14" (36cm), Jubilee II, 1989 .... 95.00
    8" (20cm) hard plastic, 1990-1992 .... 57.00
BONNIE GOES TO LONDON 8" (20cm), Scarlett Series, 1993 .... 60.00
BONNIE TODDLER 18" (46cm) cloth/hard plastic head, vinyl limbs,
    1950-1951 .... 110.00
    19" (48cm) all vinyl, 1954-1955 .... 145.00
BOONE, DANIEL 8" (20cm) hard plastic, Americana Series 60.00
BRAZIL 7" (18cm) composition, 1937-1943 .... 325.00
    9" (23cm) composition, 1938-1940 .... 250.00
    8" (20cm) hard plastic, bend knee walker, 1965-1972 .... 175.00
    bend knee 100.00
    8" (20cm) hard plastic, straight leg, 1973-1975 .... 60.00
    8" (20cm) hard plastic, straight leg, 1976-1988 .... 55.00
    1985-1987 white face 50.00
BRENDA STARR 12" (31cm) hard plastic, vinyl, 1964 .... 200.00
    Ball gown 250.00
    Beach outfit 175.00
    Bride 300.00
    Raincoat, hat, dress 250.00
    Street dresses 175.00
BRIAR ROSE 8" (20cm), MADC, 1989 (*see Special Dolls*) 350.00

A confident Madame Alexander is shown with Elsie Shaver. Madame loved her paintings, and thus created cloth dolls that resembled them in the late 1930s. *Alexander Doll Company, Bob Gantz, photographer.*

BRIDE 7" (18cm) composition, 1935-1939 .... $ 250.00
9-11" (23-28cm) composition, 1936-1941 .... 325.00
13" (33cm), 14" (36cm), 15" (38cm) composition, 1935-1941 .... 275.00
17-18" (43-46cm) composition, 1935-1943 .... 400.00
21" (53cm) composition, Royal Wedding Portrait, 1945-1947 .... 2000.00 up
21-22" (53-56cm) composition, 1942-1943 .... 585.00
   In trunk, trousseau, composition .... 1500.00 up
14" (36cm) Pink Bride, 1950 .... 750.00
18" (46cm) Pink Bride, 1950 .... 800.00-900.00
23" (58cm) hard plastic 1949, 1952-1955 .... 675.00
8" (20cm) hard plastic, Quizkin, 1953 .... 650.00 up
8" (20cm) hard plastic, 1955-1958 .... 325.00
25" (64cm) hard plastic, 1955 .... 700.00
10" (25cm) hard plastic, in trunk, trousseau, 1950s .... 900.00 up
18" (46cm) hard plastic, 1949-1955 .... 675.00
21" (53cm) hard plastic, 1949-1953 .... 875.00
15" (38cm) hard plastic, 1951-1955 .... 575.00

Mint 20in (51cm) *Jane Withers* is from the late 1930s and early 1940s. She has a mohair wig, uses a special mold, and has her signature script pin.

Cissy Brides
Lucille Ball *Forever Darling* Bride - Lace overskirt with pleated
underskirt, elaborate cap bridal veil decorated with flowers.
(This doll was made the same year as the film *Forever Darling*
with Lucille Ball and Desi Arnez.) 1955 ....$ 3000.00 up
Brocade gown appliqued bodice and skirt
"A Child's Dream Come True" Series, 1955 ....475.00
Gown has lace bodice, tulle skirt finely pleated tulle
Cap with veil "Cissy Fashion Parade" Series, 1956 ....475.00
Gown white satin bodice, double train, tulle skirt
"Cissy Models Her Formal Gowns" Series, 1957 ....500.00
Gown of fragile lace bridal, wreath pattern at bottom of skirt.
"Dolls to Remember" Series, 1958 ....575.00
21" (53cm), doll has straight arms and short neck.
Gown of nylon pleated tulle, puffed sleeves, 1959 ....500.00
21" (53cm), doll has straight arms and short neck.
Gown beige lace over skirt, pleated tulle under skirt, 1962 ....600.00

One of the most beautiful
composition dolls ever made
in the early 1940s is this 24in
(61cm) *Kate Greenaway*.
Madame brought the classic
illustrations to life.

Cissette Brides
    10" (25cm) hard plastic, gown tulle with short veil (pictured
       on the front cover of "Madame Alexander presents Cissette" -
       promotion book that came with early dolls), 1957 ....$ 275.00
    10" (25cm) hard plastic, gown tulle and bridal lace with tulle
       cap veil. (matches Cissy 1956 and Lissy 1957 Brides), 1957 ....275.00
    10" (25cm) hard plastic, gown lace bridal wreath pattern.
       (matches Cissy and Elise brides of same year), 1958 ....300.00
    10" (25cm) hard plastic, gown tulle with puffed sleeves, 1959-1960 ....275.00
    10" (25cm) hard plastic, gown tulle with rhinestones on collar
       and veil, 1961 ....275.00
    10" (25cm) hard plastic, gown has lace on bodice and lace
       trim on skirt long veil, 1962 ....275.00
    10" (25cm) hard plastic, gown tulle with rows of lace at
       bodice and hem of skirt. (matches Elise bride of same year), 1963....275.00
Lissy Brides
    12" (31cm), doll jointed at arms, elbow, knee, hip and
       shoulder. Gown tulle with tulle cap veil, 1956 ....250.00
    12" (31cm), same doll (jointed) and gown as 1956 but
       with long veil, 1957 ....250.00
    12" (31cm), jointed doll. Gown dotted net, with tulle veil, 1958 ....250.00
Elise Brides, dolls were jointed at ankle, knee,
    hip, elbow and shoulder, 1957-1964
    16½" (42cm) hard plastic, gown nylon tulle, chapel length veil, 1957 ..300.00
    16½" (42cm) hard plastic, gown tulle bridal wreath pattern
       on skirt, 1958 ....350.00

F.A.O. Schwarz store window, circa 1939, featured *Scarlet O'Hara* dolls and *Gone With the Wind* promotional items. *Alexander Doll Company, Bob Gantz, photographer.*

16½" (42cm) hard plastic, gown tulle with puffed sleeves,
  long veil, 1959 ....$ 300.00
16½" (42cm) hard plastic, gown satin, bodice has a lace bertha
  decorated with sequins and crystal beads, 1960 .... 300.00
16½" (42cm) hard plastic, gown tulle with puffed sleeves.
  Doll has short hair style, 1961 .... 300.00
16 ½" (42cm) hard plastic, gown "cobwebby" pattern lace
  on bodice and trim of tulle skirt, 1962 .... 300.00
18" (46cm) vinyl, gown tulle rows of lace at bodice and hem.
  Jacqueline hairstyle with spit curl (various hair colors), 1963 .... 350.00
18" (46cm) hard plastic/vinyl, gown white lace bodice
  and sleeves, tiers of lace on skirt, chapel length veil, white satin
  ribbon bow at waist, 1964 .... 300.00
8" (20cm) hard plastic, 1960 .... 300.00
8" (20cm), 1963-1965, bend knee walker 250.00
21" (53cm), Portrait, full lace, lace edge on veil, 1965 .... 900.00
8" (20cm), 1966-1972, bend knee 150.00
17" (43cm) plastic, vinyl, 1965-1970 .... 300.00
17" (43cm) plastic, vinyl, 1966-1971 .... 250.00
17" (43cm) plastic, vinyl, 1966-1988 .... 125.00
21" (53cm), full lace overskirt, plain veil, 1969 .... 775.00
8" (20cm), 1973-1975, straight leg 60.00

What little girl or collector would not be excited by this publicity photo taken in the early 1940s at the Alexander Doll Company showroom in New York City? The featured doll is *Wendy Ann*, one of the prettiest dolls ever produced by the Alexander Doll Company. *Alexander Doll Company, Bob Gantz, photographer.*

ELISE BRIDES continued from page 43.

14" (36cm) plastic, vinyl, 1973-1976 .... $ 75.00
8" (20cm), 1976-1992, straight leg 55.00
8" (20cm), 1985-1987, white face 45.00
14" (36cm) plastic, vinyl, Classic Dolls, 1987-1990 .... 95.00
21" (53cm) porcelain, 1989-1990 .... 510.00
10" (25cm), Portrette Series, 1990-1991 .... 100.00
12" (31cm) porcelain, 1991-1993 .... 255.00
14" (36cm), ecru gown, reintroduced 1992 .... 165.00
8" (20cm) Bride, Americana Series, 1993 .... 70.00
BRIDESMAID   9" (23cm) composition, 1937-1939 .... 325.00
11-14" (28-36cm) composition, 1938-1942 .... 350.00
15-18" (38-46cm) composition, 1939-1944 .... 375.00
20-22" (51-56cm) composition, Portrait, 1941-1947 .... 1500.00
21½" (55cm) composition, 1938-1941 .... 950.00
15-17" (38-43cm) hard plastic, 1950-1952 .... 575.00
18" (46cm) hard plastic, 1952 .... 600.00
19" (48cm) rigid vinyl, in pink, 1952-1953 .... 550.00
15" (38cm) hard plastic, 1952 .... 425.00
15" (38cm) hard plastic, 1955 .... 275.00

The name *Wendy Ann* has appeared in Alexander Doll Company listings since the 1940s. Still used today, her name symbolizes a sweet little girl who loves being loved. She is all composition with sleep eyes and a human hair wig.

18" (46cm) hard plastic, 1955 ....$ 375.00
25" (64cm) hard plastic, 1955 ....500.00
8" (20cm) hard plastic, straight leg walker, 1955 ....550.00
20" (51cm) hard plastic, 1956 ....500.00
8" (20cm), bend knee walker, 1956 ....650.00
8" (20cm), bend knee walker, 1957-1958 ....650.00
16½" (42cm) hard plastic, 1957-1959 ....425.00
10" (25cm) hard plastic, 1957-1963 ....450.00
12" (31cm) hard plastic, 1956-1959 ....425.00
17" (43cm) plastic/vinyl, 1966-1971 ....250.00
BRIGITTA   11" (28cm) & 14" (36cm), (*see Sound of Music*)
BRINKER, GRETEL   12" (31cm), 1993 ....90.00
BRINKER, HANS   12" (31cm), 1993 ....90.00
BROOKE   14" (36cm), made for FAO Schwarz, 1988 (*see Special Dolls*) 150.00
BUBBLES CLOWN   8" (20cm), Americana Series, 1993 ....50.00
BUCK RABBIT   cloth, felt, 1930s 600.00
BUD   16-19" (41-48cm) cloth/vinyl, 1952...150.00
19" & 25" (48cm & 64cm), 1952-1953 ....250.00
BULGARIA   8" (20cm), 1986-1987 ....55.00
BUMBLE BEE   8" (20cm) hard plastic, Americana Series, 1992-1993 ....50.00
BUNNY   18" (46cm) plastic/vinyl, 1962...250.00
BURMA   7" (18cm) composition, 1939-1943 ....325.00
BUTCH   14-16" (36-41cm) composition/cloth, 1949-1951 ....150.00

Baby dolls are always an Alexander favorite. The name *Genius* in one form or another is still being used today. Here is the *Little Genius* 1940s display in the Alexander New York showroom. *Alexander Doll Company, Bob Gantz, photographer.*

11-12" (28-31cm) composition/cloth, 1942-1946 .... $ 150.00
11-16" (28-41cm) hard plastic, 1949-1951 .... 150.00 up
14" (36cm) cloth, vinyl head and limbs, 1950 .... 125.00
12" (31cm) cloth/vinyl, 1965-1966 .... 75.00
BUTCH, LITTLE   9" (23cm) all vinyl, 1967-1968 .... 125.00
BUTCH MCGUFFEY   22" (56cm) composition, cloth, 1940-1941 .... 200.00

C CAMELOT IN COLUMBIA   8" (20cm), made for Columbia Show, 1991
(*see Special Dolls*) 125.00
CAMEO LADY   10" (25cm), CU, 1991 (*see Special Dolls*) 125.00
CAMILLE   21" (53cm) composition, 1938-1939 .... 2000.00 up
CANADA   8" (20cm) hard plastic, bend knee, 1968-1972 .... 115.00
straight leg, 1973-1975 .... 60.00
straight legs, 1976-1988 .... 55.00
white face, 1986 .... 55.00
CAPTAIN HOOK   8" (20cm) hard plastic, 1992-1993 .... 65.00
CAREEN   14" (36cm), Scarlett Series, 1993 .... 125.00
CARMEN
7" (18cm) composition, 1938-1943 .... 325.00
9-11" (23-28cm) composition, boy and girl, 1938-1943 .... 300.00 each
11" (28cm) composition, sleep eyes, 1937-1939 .... 350.00
11-13" (28-33cm) composition, 1937-1940 .... 475.00
15-18" (38-46cm) composition, 1939-1942 .... 675.00
21" (53cm) composition, 1939-1942 .... 1000.00
14" (36cm) plastic/vinyl, Opera Series, 1983-1986 .... 90.00
CARMEN MIRANDA PORTRETTE   1993 .... 75.00
CARNIVAL IN RIO   21" (53cm) porcelain, 1989-1990 .... 460.00
CARNIVAL IN VENICE   21" (53cm) porcelain, 1990-1991 .... 525.00
CARNVALE DOLL   21" (53cm), made for FAO Schwarz, 1991
(*see Special Dolls*) 190.00
CAROLINE   15" (38cm) vinyl, in dresses, pants, 1961-1962 .... 285.00
In boy hairstyle (possibly John Jr.), undressed 450.00

A display of composition portrait dolls in Bullucks, Wilshire, California. Some of these dolls have still not been identified. *Alexander Doll Company, Bob Gantz, photographer.*

In riding habit .... $ 350.00
In case/wardrobe .... 1400.00 up
CAROLINE 8" (20cm), made for Belk & Leggett, 1993 (*see Special Dolls*) 70.00
CARREEN 14-17" (36-43cm) composition, 1937-1938 .... 900.00
14" (36cm) plastic/vinyl, 1992-1993 .... 132.00
CARROT TOP 21" (53cm) cloth, 1967 .... 125.00
CASSOCK 8" (20cm) hard plastic, 1989-1991 .... 60.00
CENTURY OF FASHIONS 14" & 18" (36 & 46cm) hard plastic, 1954 .... 1500.00
CHARITY 8" (20cm) hard plastic, Americana Series, 1961 .... 1200.00
CHARLENE 18" (46cm) cloth, vinyl, 1991-1992 .... 105.00
CHATTERBOX 24" (61cm) plastic, vinyl, talker, 1961. .... 250.00
CHEERLEADER 8" (20cm), made for I. Magnin, 1990 (*see Special Dolls*) 65.00
8" hard plastic, black or white doll, royal blue, gold outfit,
Americana Series, 1992 .... 52.00
8" (20cm), Americana Series, 1990-1993 .... 55.00
CHERI 18" (46cm) hard plastic, white satin gown, pink opera coat,
Me and My Shadow Series, 1954 .... 1300.00
CHERRY TWINS 8" (20cm) hard plastic, 1957 only .... 900.00 up each
CHERUB 12" (31cm) vinyl, 1960-1961 .... 475.00
18" (46cm) hard plastic head, cloth & vinyl, early 1950s 350.00
CHERUB BABIES cloth, 1930s 475.00
CHILE 8" (20cm) hard plastic, 1992 .... 55.00
CHINA 7" (18cm) composition, 1936-1940 .... 250.00
9" (23cm) composition, 1935-1938 .... 265.00

Susie-Q was a popular cloth doll in Alexander Doll Company history. This great photo taken at the New York showroom shows the line in the early 1940s. *Alexander Doll Company, Bob Gantz, photographer.*

8" (20cm) hard plastic, bend knee, 1972 .... $ 95.00
8" (20cm) Smiling face 125.00
Straight leg, 1973-1975. .... 60.00
Straight legs, 1976-1986 .... 55.00
    1987-1989 .... 55.00
CHRISTENING BABY 11-13" (28-33cm) cloth,vinyl, 1951-1954 .... 75.00
    16-19" (41-48cm) 100.00
CHRISTINE 21" (53cm), one-of-a-kind, Disneyworld Auction, 1990
    (*see Special Dolls*) 5000.00
CHRISTMAS CANDY 14" (36cm), Classic Dolls, 1993 .... 100.00
CHRISTMAS CAROLING 10" (25cm), Portrette Series, 1992-1993 .... 105.00
CHRISTMAS COOKIE 14" (36cm), 1992 .... 115.00
CHURCHILL, LADY 18" (46cm) hard plastic, Beaux Arts Series, 1953 .... 1500.00
CHURCHILL, SIR WINSTON 18" (46cm) hard plastic, 1953 .... 1200.00
CINDERELLA 7-8" (18-20cm) composition, 1935-1944 .... 275.00
    9" (23cm) composition, 1936-1941 .... 350.00
    16-18" (41-46cm) composition, 1935-1939 .... 475.00 up
    14" (36cm) hard plastic, ball gown, 1950-1951 .... 700.00
    14" (36cm) hard plastic, "poor" outfit, 1950-1951 .... 650.00
    18" (46cm) hard plastic, 1950-1951 .... 675.00

Always a favorite of Alexander doll collectors, *Madeline* was an 18in (46cm) girl doll with a ball jointed body and an open-crown vinyl head with a glued-on wig. She was constructed just like an "antique" doll to show Madame's theory that dolls should be unbreakable. The design structure is uncannily like fine, old dolls.

8" (20cm) hard plastic, 1955 ....$ 950.00
12" (31cm) hard plastic, 1963. ....650.00 up
14" (36cm) plastic, vinyl, "poor" outfit, 1967-1992 ....92.00
14" (36cm) plastic, vinyl, dressed in pink, 1970-1983 ....75.00
    blue ball gown, 1984-1986..85.00
14" (36cm) Cinderella & trunk, made for Enchanted Doll House, 1985
    (*see Special Dolls*)...350.00
14" (36cm), white ball gown, Classic Dolls, 1987-1991 ....132.00
10" (25cm), Disney World®, 1989 (*see Special Dolls*) 685.00
10" (25cm), Portrette Series, 1990-1991 ....75.00
8" (20cm) hard plastic, Storyland Dolls, 1990-1993 ....55.00
8" (20cm), "poor" outfit in blue w/black strips, 1992 ....55.00
14" (36cm), white, gold ball gown, 1992 ....132.00
8" (20cm), blue ballgown, 1992-1993 ....65.00

CISSETTE   Cissette introduced in 1957. 10" (25cm) tall, high heel feet.
Jointed at the knee, hips, shoulder and neck. Prices for pristine dolls in
original costumes, including under garments and shoes. Allow more for
mint-in-box dolls, those in rare costumes and those with fancy hairdos.
    Beauty queen with trophy, 1961 ....225.00
    Coats and Hats 300.00

Made from the same mold as
Maggie, this demure 21in
(53cm) *Kate Smith's Annabelle*
is a real show stopper.

Formals ....$ 400.00
Pant Outfits 250.00
Special gift set with three wigs ....600.00 up
Street dresses 275.00

CISSY 20-21" (51-53cm) introduced with mature fashion body, jointed elbows, knees and high heel feet in 1955. The Cissy face had been used previously on other dolls. Hundreds of outfits were produced for Cissy, not all appear in the catalog reprints. The Cissy doll body is subject to seam cracks on legs and necks, one should inspect the doll carefully before purchase. Many of the dolls have lost their check color. Prices are for mint dolls, with good face color in original costumes.

1955 white organdy gown trimmed in lace and red roses 1200.00
Ball gowns 775.00
Magazine ads, 1950s 20.00
Pant Suits 300.00
Street dresses 350.00
Trunk/wardrobe 1500.00

CISSY BRIDE 1921 21" (53cm), Companions 8" (20cm), one-of-a-kind, Disneyland®⋅ 1993 (*see Special Dolls*) 6000.00

The *Maggie* series of teenage dolls was a smash hit. Madame won the Fashion Academy Award for this simplistic design. Made in all hard plastic, these dolls used one of the two hard plastic doll faces available in the early 1950s for larger size dolls. *Alexander Doll Company, Bob Gantz, Photographer.*

CISSY BY SCASSI   21" (53cm), made for FAO Schwarz, 1990
  (*see Special Dolls*) ....$ 300.00
CLARA & THE NUTCRACKER   14" (36cm) 90.00
CLARABELLE CLOWN   19" (48cm), 1951-1953 ....385.00
  29" (74cm) 600.00
  49" (124cm) 750.00
CLAUDETTE   10" (25cm), Portrette Series, 1988-1989 ....55.00
CLAUS, MRS.   8" (20cm), mid year release, 1993 ....60.00
CLAUS, SANTA   8" (20cm), mid year release, 1993 ....70.00
CLEOPATRA   12" (31cm), Portraits of History Series, 1980-1985 ....40.00
CLEVELAND, FRANCES   1985-1987, 4th set, First Ladies Series 75.00
CLOVER KID   7" (18cm) composition, 1935-1936 ....325.00
CLOWN   8" (20cm), painted face, Americana Series, 1990-1991 ....50.00
  Bobo   8" (20cm) hard plastic, 1991-1992...50.00
  Stilts   8" (20cm), 1992-1993 ....60.00
  Bubbles   8" (20cm), 1993...50.00
COCO   21" (53cm) plastic, vinyl, in clothes other than Portrait, 1966 .... 1800.00 up
  10" (25cm), Portrette Series, 1989-1992 ....55.00

An all hard plastic, early 1950s *Alice in Wonderland* gift set. The mold is the same as for *Maggie* and *Annabelle. Alexander Doll Company, Bob Gantz, Photographer.*

COLLEEN   10" (25cm), Portrette Series, 1988 .... $ 55.00
COLONIAL   7" (18cm) composition, 1937-1938 .... 265.00
   9" (23cm) composition, 1936-1939 .... 285.00
   8" (20cm) hard plastic, bend knee walker, 1962-1964 .... 365.00
COLUMBIAN SAILOR   12" (31cm), UFDC Luncheon, 1993,
   (*see Special Dolls*) 350.00
CONFEDERATE OFFICER   12" (31cm), Scarlett Series, 1990-1991 .... 80.00
   8" (20cm) hard plastic, Scarlett Series, 1992 (Ashley) 55.00
COOKIE   19" (48cm) composition, cloth, 1938-1940 .... 500.00
COOLIDGE, GRACE   14"(36cm), 6th set, First Ladies Series, 1989-1990 .... 100.00
CORNELIA   16" (41cm) cloth, felt, 1930s 700.00
   21" (53cm), dressed in pink with full cape, Portrait Series,
   1972 .... 400.00
   pink with 3/4-length jacket (green eyed), 1973 .... 350.00
   blue with black trim, 1974 .... 325.00
   rose red with black trim and hat, 1975 .... 325.00
   pink with black trim and hat, 1976 .... 300.00
   blue with full cape, 1978 .... 275.00
COUNTRY CHRISTMAS   14" (36cm), Classic Dolls, 1991-1992 .... 132.00

Often thought to be a Disneyland® Exclusive, a 10in (25cm), special mold *Walt Disney's® Sleeping Beauty* is the picture of hard plastic perfection. Sold in such diverse places as SS Kressege's Five and Ten to Spiegel's, the Disney® heroine came in a 16in (41cm) and a 21in (53cm) size as well. The 21in (53cm) size also used a special mold.

COUNTRY COUSIN   10" (25cm) cloth, 1940s .... $ 850.00
   16½" (42cm) vinyl, 1958 .... 400.00
COURTNEY AND FRIENDS   8" (20cm) hard plastic, Alexander and 26" (66cm)
   porcelain, Gunzel, 1992 (*see Special Dolls*) 850.00
COUSIN GRACE   8" (20cm) hard plastic, bend knee walker, 1957 .... 1200.00
COUSIN KAREN   8" (20cm) hard plastic, bend knee walker, 1956 .... 1200.00
COWARDLY LION   8" (20cm), Storyland Dolls, 1993 .... 55.00
COWBOY   8" (20cm) hard plastic, bend knee, Americana Series,
   1967-1969 .... 350.00
   8" (20cm), MADC, 1987 (*see Special Dolls*) 500.00
COWGIRL   8" (20cm) hard plastic, bend knee, Americana and Storyland
   Dolls, 1967-1979 .... 350.00
   10" (25cm), Portrette Series, 1990-1991 .... 65.00
CRETE   8" (20cm) straight leg, 1987 .... 45.00
CROCKETT, DAVY BOY OR GIRL   8" (20cm) hard plastic, 1955 .... 650.00
CRY DOLLY   14-16" (36-41cm) vinyl, 1953 .... 175.00
   14" (36cm), 16" (41cm), 19" (48cm), swimsuit 125.00
   16-19" (41-48cm) all vinyl, dress or rompers 145.00

Called the quintessential pre-pubescent face, this all vinyl *Pollyanna* utilized the molds first used on *Mary-Bell Gets Well*. This face mold is a favorite with collectors.

CUDDLY   10½" (27cm) cloth, 1942-1944 .... $ 325.00
    17" (43cm) cloth, 1942-1944 .... 375.00
CURLY LOCKS   8" (20cm) hard plastic, 1955 .... 850.00 up
    8" (20cm) straight leg, Storyland Dolls, 1987-1988 .... 70.00
CYNTHIA   15" (38cm) hard plastic, black hard plastic, 1952 .... 750.00 up
    18" (46cm), 1952 .... 950.00 up
    23" (58cm), 1952 .... 1200.00 up
CZECHOSLOVAKIA   7" (18cm) composition, 1935-1937 .... 250.00
    8" (20cm) hard plastic, bend knee, 1972 .... 135.00
    straight leg, 1973-1975 .... 45.00
    straight leg, 1976-1987 .... 45.00
    8" (20cm) white face, 1985-1987 .... 45.00
    8" (20cm), re-introduced 1992-1993 .... 55.00

D DAFFY DOWN DILLEY   8" (20cm) straight legs, Storyland Dolls, 1986 ... 60.00
    8" (20cm), Storyland Dolls, 1987-1989 .... 55.00
    DAISY   10" (25cm), Portrette Series, 1987-1989 .... 50.00
DANISH   7" (18cm) composition, 1937-1941 .... 325.00
    9" (23cm) composition, 1938-1940 .... 350.00
DARE, VIRGINIA   9" (23cm) composition, 1940-1941 .... 350.00

Photograph of the doll named *Miss Liberty.* She was made in the early 1950s and given to a young lady named Dace Epermanis, the 150,000th displaced person on record to enter the United States. Possibly one-of-a-kind. *Alexander Doll Company, Bob Gantz, photographer.*

Darlene 18" (46cm) cloth, vinyl, 1991-1992 .... $ 105.00

Darling, Mrs. 10" (25cm), #1165, Portrettes, 1993 .... 100.00

David & Diana 8" (20cm), made for FAO Schwarz, 1989
(*see Special Dolls*) 195.00

David Copperfield 16" (41cm) cloth, Dicken's character, early 1930s 800.00
7" (18cm) composition, 1936-1938 .... 350.00
14" (36cm) composition, 1938 .... 750.00

David Quack-A-Field or Twistail cloth, felt, 1930s 750.00

David, the Little Rabbi 8" (20cm), made for Celia's Dolls, 1991
(*see Special Dolls*) 85.00

Day of Week Dolls 7" (18cm) composition, 1935-1940 .... 325.00
9-11" (23-28cm) composition, 1936-1938 .... 350.00
13" (33cm) composition, 1939 .... 450.00

Dearest 12" (31cm) vinyl baby, 1962-1964 .... 125.00

December 14" (36cm), Classic Dolls, 1989 .... 95.00

DeFoe, Dr. 14" (36cm) composition, 1937-1939 .... 1400.00

Degas 21" (53cm) composition, Portrait, 1945-1946 .... 1900.00 up

Degas Girl 14" (36cm) plastic, vinyl, Portrait Children &
Fine Art Series, 1967-1987 .... 75.00

Freedom, another possibly one-of-a-kind all hard plastic doll, given to the same young lady. It would be interesting to know where the dolls are today. *Alexander Doll Company, Bob Gantz, photographer.*

DENMARK 10" (25cm) hard plastic, 1962-1963 .... $ 700.00

8" (20cm) hard plastic, bend knee, 1970-1972 .... 145.00

8" (20cm) hard plastic, straight leg, 1973-1975 .... 60.00

8" (20cm) hard plastic, straight leg, 1976-1989, (1985-1987 white face) 55.00

8" (20cm), re-introduced 1991 .... 55.00

DIAMOND LIL 10" (25cm), MADC, 1993 *(see Special Dolls)* 300.00

DIANA'S TEA DRESS 14" (36cm), Anne of Green Gables, 1993
(doll and tea set) 115.00

DIANA'S TRUNK SET Anne of Green Gables, 1993 (doll and wardrobe) 250.00

DICKINSON, EMILY 14" (36cm), Classic Dolls, 1989 .... 90.00

DICKSIE & DUCKSIE cloth, felt, 1930s 600.00

DILLY DALLY SALLY 7" (18cm) composition, 1937-1942 .... 325.00

9" (23cm) composition, 1938-1939 .... 350.00

DING DONG DELL 7" (18cm) composition, 1937-1942 .... 325.00

DINNER AT EIGHT 10" (25cm), Portrette Series, 1989-1991 .... 60.00

DINOSAUR 8" (20cm), Americana Series, 1993 .... 50.00

DIONNE QUINTS Original mint or very slight craze.

8" (20cm) composition toddlers, molded hair and painted eyes,
1935-1939 .... 175.00 each, 1200.00 set

The face of the 1953 *Wendy*, part of the Alexander Doll Company miniature doll line, nicknamed "Alexanderkins." This doll would become a staple to this day for fine collections.

8" (20cm) composition toddlers, wigs and painted eyes,
1938-1939 ....$ 175.00 each, 1200.00 set
11" (28cm) composition toddlers, wigs and sleep eyes,
1935-1938 ....350.00 each, 2000.00 set
11" (28cm) composition toddlers, molded hair and sleep eyes,
1937-1938 ....350.00 each, 2000.00 set
11" (28cm) composition babies, wigs and sleep eyes,
1936 ....300.00 each, 2000.00 set
11" (28cm) composition babies, molded hair and sleep
eyes, 1936 ....300.00 each, 2000.00 set
14" (36cm) composition toddlers, 1937-1938 ....425.00 each, 2450.00 set
14" (36cm) cloth body, composition, 1938 ....500.00 each, 3200.00 set
16" (41cm) all cloth, 1935-1936 ....800.00
16-17" (41-43cm) composition toddlers, 1937-1939 ....625.00 each, 3600.00 set
17" (43cm) cloth body, composition, 1938 ....550.00 each, 3500.00 set
19" (48cm) composition toddlers, 1936-1938 ....700.00 each, 4200.00 set
20" (51cm) composition toddlers, 1938-1939 ....700.00 each, 4200.00 set
22" (56cm) cloth, composition, 1936-1937 ....675.00
24" (61cm) all cloth, 1935-1936 ....1200.00
DOLLS OF THE MONTH 7-8" (18-20cm) composition, 1936-1938 ....245.00 each

In 1954 the hit news was that *Wendy* could walk. Trying to stay current, the new 8in (20cm) dolls could gently be led by the hand to walk. The wrist tags called the doll *Wendy-Ann Walker*.

DOLLY   8" (20cm), Storyland Dolls, 1988-1989 ....$ 45.00
DOMINICAN REPUBLIC   8" (20cm) straight leg, 1986-1988
   (1985-1986 white face) 45.00
DOROTHY   8" (20cm) hard plastic, 1991-1993 ....52.00
   14" (36cm), all blue, white check dress, 1990-1993 ....84.00
DOTTIE DUMBUNNIE   cloth, felt, 1930s ....800.00 up
DRESSED FOR THE OPERA   18" (46cm) hard plastic, 1953 ....1500.00
DRUCILLA   14" (36cm), MADC, 1992 (see Special Dolls) ....S/A
DRUM MAJORETTE   7½" (19cm) hard plastic, 1955 ....900.00
DUDE RANCH   8" (20cm) hard plastic, 1955.................................700.00
DUMPLIN' BABY   20-23½" (51-60cm), 1957-1958 ....250.00
DUTCH   7" (18cm) composition, 1935-1939 ....325.00
   9" (23cm) composition boy or girl, 1936-1941 ....350.00
   8" (20cm) hard plastic boy*, bend knee walker, 1964.................150.00
   bend knee, 1965-1972..60.00-125.00
   8" (20cm) hard plastic, straight leg, 1972-1973..........................45.00
   8" (20cm) hard plastic girl*, bend knee walker, 1961-1964.........150.00
   8" (20cm) hard plastic, bend knee, 1965-1972 ....60.00-125.00
   8" (20cm) bend knee walker, smile face, 1964 ....175.00
*Both became Netherland in 1974

E
   EASTER BONNET   14" (36cm), 1992 ....145.00
   EASTER BUNNY   8" (20cm), made for A Child at Heart, 1991
      (see Special Dolls) 250.00
EASTER DOLL   8" (20cm) hard plastic, 1968 ....1200.00
   14" (36cm) plastic/vinyl, 1968...750.00
EASTER SUNDAY   8" (20cm), black or white, Americana Series, 1993..............60.00
ECUADOR   8" (20cm) hard plastic, bend knee and bend knee walker,
   1963-1966 ....350.00
EDITH, THE LONELY DOLL   8" (20cm) hard plastic, 1958 ....500.00
   16" (41cm) plastic, vinyl, 1958-1959 ....245.00
   22" (56cm), 1958-1959 ....325.00
EDITH WITH GOLDEN HAIR   18" (46cm) cloth, 1940s 600.00
EDWARDIAN   "so-called" 8" (20cm) hard plastic, 1953 ....950.00
   "so-called" 18" (46cm) hard plastic, Glamour Girl Series, 1953 ....1200.00
EISENHOWER, MAMIE   14" (36cm), 6th set, First Ladies Series, 1989-1990 ...100.00
EGYPT   8" (20cm) straight leg, 1986-1989 ....55.00
EGYPTIAN   7-8" (18-20cm) composition, 1936-1940.....................325.00
   9" (23cm) composition, 1936-1940 ....350.00
ELAINE   8" (20cm) hard plastic, matches 18" (46cm), 1954 ....1200.00
   18" (46cm) hard plastic, blue organdy dress, Me and My Shadow
   Series, 1954 ....1500.00
ELISE   16½" (42cm) hard plastic, vinyl arms, jointed ankles and knees,
   1957-1964.
      Ballerina 350.00
      In ball gown 600.00
      In street clothes 300.00
      With vinyl head, 1962 ....325.00
   14" (36cm) plastic, vinyl, 1988 ....75.00
   17" (43cm) hard plastic, vinyl one-piece arms and legs, jointed ankles
      and knees, 1961-1962 ....200.00
   17" (43cm) plastic, vinyl, street dress, 1966 ....200.00
   17" (43cm) in trunk, trousseau, 1966-1972 ....750.00
   17" (43cm) Portrait, 1972-1973 ....175.00
   17" (43cm) in formal, 1966, 1976-1977 ....175.00

17" (43cm) Bride, 1966-1987 ....$ 175.00
17" (43cm) Ballerina, 1966-1991 ....75.00
17" (43cm) Elise in discontinued costumes, 1966-1989 ....150.00 up
18" (46cm) with bouffant hairstyle, 1963 ....300.00
18" (46cm) hard plastic, vinyl, jointed ankles and knees, 1963-1964 ....200.00
    In riding habit 350.00
ELIZA   14" (36cm), Classic Dolls, 1991 ....155.00
EMILY   cloth, felt, 1930s 700.00
EMPEROR & NIGHTINGALE   one-of-a-kind, 1992 Disney World® Auction,
    (*see Special Dolls*) 5200.00
EMPRESS ELISABETH   10" (25cm), made for My Doll House, 1991
    (*see Special Dolls*) 140.00
ENCHANTED DOLL   (*see Special Dolls*)
    8" (20cm), rick-rack on pinafore, lace trim, 1980....................................300.00
    8" (20cm), eyelet pinafore, eyelet trim, 1981 ....325.00
    10" (25cm) hard plastic, 1988 (*see Special Dolls*) ....250.00 up
ENCHANTED EVENING   21" (53cm) Portrait, 1991 (uses vinyl *Cissy* mold) 200.00
ENGLISH GUARD   8" (20cm) hard plastic, bend knee, 1966-1968 ....250.00
    8" (20cm), reintroduced 1989-1991 ....55.00
ESKIMO   9" (23cm) composition, 1936-1939 ....265.00
    8" (20cm) hard plastic, bend knee, Americana Series, 1967-1969 ....350.00
    With smile face 400.00
ESTONIA   8" (20cm) straight leg, 1986-1987 ....75.00
EVA LOVELACE   7" (18cm) composition, 1935 ....325.00
    Cloth, 1935 ....600.00
EVANGELINE   18" (46cm) cloth, 1930s ....700.00 up

F   FAIRY GODMOTHER   Outfit, MADC, 1983 (not
    an Alexander outfit) 400.00
    14" (36cm), Classic Dolls, 1983-1992 ....75.00-165.00
10" (25cm) Portrettes, 1993 ....85.00
FAIRY PRINCESS   7-8" (18-20cm) composition, 1940-1943 ....285.00
    9" (23cm) composition, 1939-1941 ....300.00
    11" (28cm) composition, 1939 ....350.00
    15-18" (38-46cm) composition, 1939-1942 ....600.00
    21-22" (53-56cm) composition, 1939, 1944-1946 ....950.00
FAIRY QUEEN   14½" (37cm) composition, 1940-1946 ....600.00
    18" (46cm) composition, 1940-1946 ....750.00
    14½" (37cm) hard plastic, 1948-1950..675.00
    18" (46cm) hard plastic, 1949-1950 ....885.00
FAIRY TALES - DUMAS   9" (23cm) composition, 1937-1941 ....300.00
FAITH   8" (20cm) hard plastic, Americana Group, 1961 ....1200.00 up
    8" (20cm) hard plastic, CU Gathering, 1992 (*see Special Dolls*) 225.00
FANNIE ELIZABETH   8" (20cm), made for Belk & Leggett, 1991
    (*see Special Dolls*) 75.00
FARMER'S DAUGHTER   8" (20cm), made for Enchanted Doll House, 1991
    (*see Special Dolls*) 150.00
FARMER'S DAUGHTER Goes to Town   cape and basket added,
    made for Enchanted Doll House, 1992 (*see Special Dolls*) 90.00
FASHIONS OF THE CENTURY   14-18" (36-46cm) hard plastic, 1954-1955 ......1500.00
FILLMORE, ABIGAIL   3rd set, First Ladies Series, 1982-1984 ....75.00
FINDLAY, JANE   1st set, First Ladies Series, 1979-1981 ....100.00
FINLAND   8" (20cm) hard plastic, bend knee, 1968-1972 ....125.00
    8" (20cm) hard plastic, straight leg, 1973-1975..60.00
    8" (20cm) hard plastic, straight leg, 1976-1987 ....45.00

Finnish 7" (18cm) composition, 1935-1937 .... $ 245.00
First Communion 8" (20cm) hard plastic, 1957 .... 650.00
 14" (36cm), Classic Dolls, 1991-1992 .... 95.00
First Ladies
 1st set, 1976-1978 .... 700.00 set
 2nd set, 1979-1981 .... 550.00 set
 3rd set, 1982-1984 .... 475.00 set
 4th set, 1985-1987 .... 550.00 set
 5th set, 1988 .... 475.00 set
 6th set, 1989-1990 .... 600.00 set
Fisher Quints (so called) 7" (18cm) hard plastic, vinyl, 1964 set 400.00
Five Little Peppers 13" (33cm) & 16" (41cm) composition, 1936 .... 600.00 each
Flapper 10" (25cm), Portrette Series, 1988-1991 .... 50.00
 10" (25cm), MADC, 1988 (*see Special Dolls*) 200.00
Flora McFlimsey 9" (23cm) composition, 1938-1941 .... 300.00
 14" (36cm) composition, 1938-1944 .... 450.00
 15-16" (38-41cm) composition, 1938-1944 .... 500.00
 16-17" (41-43cm) composition, 1936-1937 .... 500.00
 22" (56cm) composition, 1938-1944 .... 700.00
 15" (38cm) Miss Flora McFlimsey, vinyl head, 1953 .... 575.00
Flowergirl 16-18" (41-46cm) composition, 1939, 1944-1947 .... 550.00
 20-24" (51-61cm) composition, 1939, 1944-1947 .... 750.00

Mint-in-box dolls, such as this perfect *Wendy* dressed for a visit to a Dude Ranch, are practically impossible to find today and would bring a premium price above list.

15" (38cm) hard plastic, 1954	$ 600.00
15-18" (38-46cm) hard plastic, 1954	425.00
8" (20cm) hard plastic, 1956	650.00
10" (25cm), Portrette Series, 1988-1990	55.00
8" (20cm) hard plastic, black or white doll, Americana Series, 1992	55.00

FRANCE   7" (18cm) composition, 1936-1943 .... 265.00
FRENCH   9" (23cm) composition, 1937-1941 .... 265.00
    8" (20cm) hard plastic, bend knee walker, 1961-1965 .... 150.00
    8" (20cm) hard plastic, bend knee, 1965-1972 .... 135.00
    8" (20cm) hard plastic, straight leg, 1973-1975 .... 60.00
    white face, 1985 .... 55.00
    8" (20cm) straight leg, 1976-1992 .... 52.00
FRENCH ARISTOCRAT   10" (25cm) Portrette, 1991 .... 105.00
FRENCH FLOWERGIRL   8" (20cm) hard plastic, 1956 .... 650.00
FRIAR TUCK   8" (20cm) hard plastic, 1989-1991 .... 45.00
FRIEDRICH   (*see Sound of Music*)
FROU-FROU   40" (101cm) all cloth, yarn hair, ballerina in green, lilac,
    1951 only 700.00
FUNNY   18" (46cm) cloth, 1963-1977 .... 50.00

Madame Alexander's design skills are shown with the perfect scale print for this 1950s *Wendy.*

G GAINSBOROUGH   10" (25cm), pink, full dress, hat, 1957 ....$ 425.00

20" (51cm) hard plastic, taffeta gown, picture hat, Models
Formals Series, 1957 .... 1000.00
21" (53cm) hard plastic, vinyl arms, blue with white lace jacket, 1968 .... 650.00
21" (53cm), bright blue with full ecru overlace, 1972 .... 550.00
21" (53cm), pale blue, scallop lace overskirt, 1973 .... 475.00
21" (53cm), pink with full lace overdress, 1978 .... 350.00

GARDEN PARTY   18" (46cm) hard plastic, 1953 .... 1200.00
8" (20cm) hard plastic, 1955 .... 800.00
20" (51cm) hard plastic, 1956-1957 .... 875.00

GARFIELD, LUCRETIA   4th set, First Ladies Series, 1985-1987 .... 90.00

GENIUS BABY   21-30" (53-76cm) plastic, vinyl, flirty eyes, 1960-1961 .... 150.00
Little,   8" (20cm) hard plastic head, vinyl, 1956-1962 (see Little Genius)

GEPPETTO   8" (20cm), Storyland Dolls, 1993 .... 45.00

GERANIUM   9" (23cm) early vinyl toddler, red organdy
dress and bonnet, 1953 .... 95.00

GERMAN (GERMANY)   8" (20cm) hard plastic, bend knee, 1966-1972 .... 125.00
8" (20cm) hard plastic, straight leg, 1973-1975 .... 60.00
8" (20cm) white face, 1986 .... 55.00
8" (20cm) straight legs, 1976-1991 .... 55.00

GIBSON GIRL   16" (41cm) cloth, 1930s 775.00
10" (25cm) hard plastic, eye shadow, 1962 .... 600.00
plain blouse with no stripes, 1963 .... 600.00 up
10" (25cm), Portrette Series, 1988-1990 .... 60.00

GIDGET   14" (36cm) plastic, vinyl, 1966 .... 325.00

GIGI   14" (36cm), Classic Dolls, 1986-1987 .... 75.00

GLAMOUR GIRLS   18" (46cm) hard plastic, 1953 .... 1250.00

GLENDA, THE GOOD WITCH   8" (20cm), Storyland Dolls, 1992-1993 .... 60.00

GODEY   21" (53cm) composition, 1945-1947 .... 1200.00
20" (51cm) hard plastic, 1951 .... 1500.00
14" (36cm) hard plastic, 1950-1951 .... 1200.00
18" (46cm) hard plastic, Glamour Girl Series, 1953 .... 1300.00
8" (20cm) straight leg walker, 1955 .... 1200.00
21" (53cm) hard plastic, vinyl straight arms, red faille gown
matching coat, black braid trim coat has black marabou's collar,
straw hat, 1960 .... 900.00
21" (53cm) hard plastic, vinyl straight arms, lavender purple
hat and coat, 1961 .... 1200.00
21" (53cm), dressed in all red, blonde hair, 1965 .... 625.00
21" (53cm) plastic, vinyl, red with black short jacket and hat, 1966 .... 2000.00
21" (53cm) hard plastic, vinyl arms, dressed in pink & ecru, 1967 .... 575.00
10" (25cm) hard plastic, dressed in all pink with bows down front, 1968 ..... 450.00
10" (25cm), all yellow with bows down front, 1969 .... 450.00
21" (53cm), red with black trim, 1969 .... 475.00
10" (25cm), all lace pink dress with natural straw hat, 1970 .... 500.00
21" (53cm), pink with burgundy short jacket, 1970 .... 325.00
21" (53cm), pink, black trim, short jacket, 1971 .... 350.00
21" (53cm), ecru with red jacket and bonnet, 1977 .... 325.00

GODEY BRIDE   14" (36cm) hard plastic, 1950 .... 875.00
18" (46cm) hard plastic, 1950-1951 .... 950.00

GODEY GROOM   14" (36cm) hard plastic, 1950 .... 900.00
18" (46cm) hard plastic, 1950-1951 .... 1500.00

GODEY LADY   14" (36cm) hard plastic, 1950 .... 950.00
18" (46cm) hard plastic, 1950-1951 .... 1500.00

GOLD RUSH   10" (25cm) hard plastic, 1963 .... 1500.00

GOLDFISH   8" (20cm), Americana Series, 1993 .... $ 70.00
GOLDILOCKS   18" (46cm) cloth, 1930s 750.00
    7-8" (18-20cm) composition, 1938-1942 .... 275.00
    14" (36cm) plastic, vinyl, satin dress, Classic Dolls, 1978-1979 .... 75.00
    14" (36cm), cotton dress, 1980-1983 .... 75.00
    8" (20cm), Storyland Dolls, 1990-1991 (1991 dress is different plaid) 55.00
    14" (36cm), long side curls, Classic Dolls, 1991 .... 95.00
GONE WITH THE WIND   14" (36cm), all white dress/green sash, 1968-1986 ..... 90.00 up
GOOD FAIRY   14" (36cm) hard plastic 675.00
GOOD LITTLE GIRL   16" (41cm) cloth, wears pink dress, mate to
    "Bad Little Girl," 1966 .... 90.00
GOYA   8" (20cm) hard plastic, 1953 .... 950.00
    21" (53cm) hard plastic, vinyl arms, multi-tier pink dress, 1968 .... 550.00
    21" (53cm), maroon dress with black Spanish lace, 1982-1983 .... 200.00
GRADUATION   8" (20cm) hard plastic, 1957 .... 800.00
    12" (31cm) hard plastic, 1957 .... 800.00
    8" (20cm), white doll, Americana Series, 1990-1992 .... 55.00
    8" (20cm), white or black doll, 1991-1992 .... 55.00
GRANDMA JANE   14" (36cm) plastic, vinyl, 1970-1972 .... 225.00
GRANT, JULIA   3rd set, First Ladies Series, 1982-1984 .... 75.00
GRAVE, ALICE   18" (46cm) cloth, 1930s 650.00
GREAT BRITAIN   8" (20cm) hard plastic, 1977-1988 .... 45.00
GREECE   8" (20cm), International Dolls, 1993 .... 47.00
GREECE (BOY)   8" (20cm) hard plastic, 1992 .... 52.00
GREEK BOY   8" (20cm) hard plastic, bend knee walker,
    1965 .... 400.00
    bend knee, 1966-1968 .... 325.00
GREEK GIRL   8" (20cm) hard plastic, bend knee, 1968-1972 .... 100.00
    8" (20cm) hard plastic, straight leg, 1973-1975 .... 60.00
    8" (20cm) hard plastic, straight leg, 1976-1987 .... 55.00
GRETEL   7" composition, 1935-1942 .... 275.00
    9" (23cm) composition, 1938-1940 .... 300.00
    7½-8" (19-20cm) hard plastic, straight leg walker, 1955 .... 500.00
    18" (46cm) hard plastic, 1948 .... 995.00 up
    8" (20cm) hard plastic, bend knee, Storyland Dolls, 1966-1972 .... 135.00
    8" (20cm) hard plastic, straight leg, 1973-1975, ... 60.00
    8" (20cm) hard plastic, straight leg, 1976-1986 .... 55.00
    8" (20cm) hard plastic, Storyland Dolls, re-introduced 50.00
GRETL   (see Sound of Music)
GROOM   18-21" (46-53cm) composition, 1946-1947 .... 900.00
    18-21" (46-53cm) hard plastic, 1949-1951 .... 800.00 up
    7½" (19cm) hard plastic, 1953-1955 .... 425.00
    14-16" (36-41cm) hard plastic, 1949-1951 .... 800.00 up
    8" (20cm) hard plastic, 1961-1963 .... 350.00
    8" (20cm), re-introduced 1989-1993 .... 60.00
GUENIVERE   10" (25cm), Portrette Series, 1992 .... 95.00

H HALLOWEEN   8" (20cm), made for Greenville Show, 1990
    (see Special Dolls) 145.00
    HAMLET   12" (31cm), Romance Collection 95.00
    12" (31cm) #1312, 1993 .... 90.00
HANSEL   7" (18cm) composition, 1935-1942 .... 285.00
    9" (23cm) composition, 1938-1940 .... 300.00
    18" (46cm) hard plastic, 1948 .... 675.00
    8" (20cm) hard plastic, straight leg walker, 1955 .... 500.00

Beautiful *Wendy* skater from the late 1950s is an example of a mint collector's doll.

HANSEL continued from page 63.

8" (20cm) hard plastic, bend knee, Storyland Dolls, 1966-1972 ....$ 135.00
8" (20cm) hard plastic, straight leg, 1973-1975...60.00
8" (20cm) hard plastic, straight leg, 1976-1986...55.00
8" (20cm) hard plastic, Storyland Dolls, re-introduced 1991-1992 ....52.00

HAPPY   20" (51cm) cloth, vinyl, 1970 ....200.00

HAPPY BIRTHDAY   8" (20cm) hard plastic, black or white doll,
Americana Series, 1992-1993 ....50.00

HAPPY BIRTHDAY BILLY   8" (20cm), black or white, Americana Series,
1993...55.00

HAPPY BIRTHDAY Madame   8" (20cm), MADC, 1985 (*see Special Dolls*) ...365.00

HARDING, FLORENCE   5th set, First Ladies Series, 1988 ....85.00

HARMONY   21" (53cm) porcelain, with 8" (20cm) hard plastic, Alexander,
nymph, one-of-a-kind by Hildegard Gunzel, Disney World® Auction,1992
(*see Special Dolls*) 7500.00

HARRISON, CAROLINE   4th set, First Ladies Series, 1985-1987 ....90.00

HAWAII   8" (20cm), Americana Series, 1990-1991 ....55.00

HAWAIIAN   7" (18cm) composition, 1936-1939 ....285.00
9" (23cm) composition, 1937-1944 ....325.00
8" (20cm) hard plastic, bend knee, Americana Series, 1966-1969 ....400.00

HAYES, LUCY   4th set, First Ladies Series, 1985-1987 ....90.00

HEATHER   18" (46cm) cloth, vinyl, 1990-1993 ....85.00

Yes, this is the right oversized purse for this mint,
incredible *Wendy*!

HEIDI 7" (18cm) composition, 1938-1939 ....$ 275.00
    14" (36cm) plastic, vinyl, Classic Dolls, 1969-1988 ....75.00
    8" (20cm) hard plastic, Storyland Dolls, 1991-1992 ....55.00
HELLO BABY 22" (56cm), 1962...145.00
HENIE, SONJA 7" (18cm) composition, 1939-1942 ....350.00
    9" (23cm) composition, 1940-1941 ....450.00
    11" (28cm) composition..550.00
    13-15" (33-38cm) composition, 1939-1942...575.00
    14" (36cm) composition 500.00-600.00
    14" (36cm) in case, wardrobe .... 1000.00 up
    17-18" (43-46cm) composition..600.00-700.00
    20-23" (51-58cm) composition..700.00-800.00
    13-14" (33-36cm) composition, jointed waist 600.00-700.00
    15-18" (38-46cm) hard plastic, vinyl, no extra joints, 1951 only 800.00
HIAWATHA 18" (46cm) cloth, early 1930s 650.00
    7" (18cm) composition...285.00
    8" (20cm) hard plastic, Americana Series, 1967-1969 ....350.00
HIGHLAND FLING 8" (20cm) hard plastic, 1955 ....500.00
HOLIDAY ON ICE 8" (20cm) hard plastic, 1992 (some tagged *Christmas on Ice*) 55.00
HOLLAND 7" (18cm) composition, 1936-1943 ....245.00
HOLLY 10" (25cm), Portrette Series, 1990-1991 ....85.00

The name *Binnie Walker* would be famous not only for the 24in (61cm) child doll shown here, but because her face would be duplicated and put on an adult doll body that would make fashion history with *Cissy*, Madame's entry into the high-heel doll world. *Alexander Doll Company, Bob Gantz, photographer.*

HOMECOMING   8" (20cm) hard plastic, MADC, 1993 (*see Special Dolls*) .$ 150.00
HONEYBEA   12" (31cm) vinyl, 1963 .... 150.00 up
HONEYBUN   18-19" (46-48cm) cloth, vinyl, 1951-1952 .... 175.00
     23-26" (58-66cm) 250.00
HONEYETTE BABY   7" (18cm) composition, little girl dress, 1934-1937 .... 285.00
     16" (41cm) composition, cloth, 1941-1942 .... 175.00
HOOVER, LOU   14" (36cm) plastic, 6th set, First Ladies Series, 1989-1990 ... 100.00
HOPE   8" (20cm), CU Gathering, 1993 (*see Special Dolls*)............................ 250.00
HUCKLEBERRY FINN   8" (20cm) hard plastic, Storyland Dolls, 1989-1991 .... 60.00
HUGGUMS, BIG   Lively, 25" (64cm), knob moves head and limbs, 1963 ...... 125.00
     25" (64cm), boy or girl, 1963-1979 .... 95.00
HUGGUMS, LITTLE   12" (31cm) rooted hair, 1963-1982, 1988 .... 55.00
     12" (31cm) molded hair, 1963-1992 .... 55.00
     14" (36cm), molded hair, 1986 .... 50.00
     12" (31cm), special outfits for Imaginarium Shop, 1991 .... 50.00-55.00
HULDA   18" (46cm), hard plastic, 1947 .... 1500.00 up
HUNGARIAN (HUNGARY)   8" (20cm) hard plastic, bend knee walker,
     1962-1965 .... 175.00
     bend knee or bend knee walker with metal crown 150.00
     bend knee, 1965-1972 .... 135.00
     8" (20cm) hard plastic, straight leg, 1973-1976.. 60.00
     8" (20cm) hard plastic, straight leg, 1976-1986.. 55.00
     8" (20cm) hard plastic, re-introduced 1992-1993 .... 50.00

Alexander Doll Company
publicity shot showing a
group of Portrait dolls that
use the *Cissy* head mold.
They are stunning cre-
ations from the golden age
of   collectible   dolls.
*Alexander Doll Company,
Bob Gantz, photographer.*

I IBIZA 8" (20cm), 1989 .... $ 90.00
ICE SKATER   8" (20cm), bend knee and bend knee walker, 1955-1956 ...... 550.00
   8" (20cm), Americana Series, 1990-1991 .... 60.00
ICELAND   10" (25cm), 1962-1963 .... 700.00 up
INDIA 8" (20cm) hard plastic, bend knee walker, 1965 .... 225.00
   8" (20cm) hard plastic, bend knee, 1965-1972 .... 135.00
   8" (20cm) hard plastic, bend knee and bend knee walker, white 135.00
   8" (20cm) hard plastic, straight leg, 1973-1975 .... 60.00
   8" (20cm) hard plastic, straight leg, 1976-1988 .... 55.00
INDIAN BOY   8" (20cm) hard plastic, bend knee, Americana Series, 1966 ..... 350.00
INDIAN GIRL   8" (20cm) hard plastic, bend knee, Americana Series, 1966 .... 400.00
INDONESIA   8" (20cm) hard plastic, bend knee, 1970-1972 .... 150.00
   With smile face, bend knee, 1970s (some years) 200.00
   8" (20cm) hard plastic, straight leg, 1972-1975 .... 60.00
   8" (20cm) hard plastic, straight leg, 1976-1988 .... 55.00
INGALLS, LAURA   14" (36cm), Classic Dolls, 1989-1991 .... 85.00
INGRES   14" (36cm) plastic, vinyl, Fine Arts Series, 1987 .... 75.00
IRIS   10" (25cm) hard plastic, 1987-1988 .... 75.00
IRISH (IRELAND)   8" (20cm) hard plastic, bend knee walker, 1965 .... 185.00
   8" (20cm) bend knee, gown, 1966-1972 .... 135.00

Cissy, a hard plastic and vinyl 21in (53cm) fashion doll, was the elite of the teen-age high heel dolls.

8" (20cm) straight leg, gown, 1973-1975 .... $ 60.00
8" (20cm) straight leg, 1976-1985 .... 55.00
8" (20cm) straight leg, 1985-1987 .... 55.00
8" (20cm) straight leg, short dress, 1987-1992 .... 50.00
ISOLDE   14" (36cm), Opera Series, 1985-1986 .... 90.00
ISRAEL   8" (20cm) hard plastic, bend knee, 1965-1972 .... 125.00
8" (20cm) hard plastic, straight leg, 1973-1975 .... 60.00
8" (20cm) hard plastic, straight leg, 1976-1989 .... 55.00
ITALY   8" (20cm) hard plastic, bend knee walker, 1961-1965 .... 150.00
8" (20cm) hard plastic, bend knee, 1965-1972 .... 135.00
8" (20cm) hard plastic, straight leg, 1973-1975 .... 60.00
white face, 1985 .... 55.00
8" (20cm) straight leg, 1976-1993 .... 55.00
ITS A GIRL   21" (53cm) hard plastic and vinyl and 8" (20cm) hard plastic
baby, one-of-a-kind, Disney World® Auction, 1992
(*see Special Dolls*) 13,500.00

J   **JACK AND JILL**   7" (18cm) composition, 1938-1943 .... 285.00 each
9" (23cm) composition, 1939 .... 300.00 each
8" (20cm) straight leg, Storyland Dolls, 1987-1992 .... 52.00 each

Very rare 1953 8in (20cm) *Coronation Queen Elizabeth II*. Shown with her lace-trimmed dress in the one-page catalog for the miniature doll line. She is a strung doll with a Tosca wig.

JACK BE NIMBLE 8" (20cm) hard plastic, made for Dolly Dears, 1993
  (*see Special Dolls*) .... $ 150.00
JACKSON, SARAH 2nd set, First Ladies Series, 1979-1981 .... 105.00
JACQUELINE 21" (53cm) hard plastic,vinyl arms, street dress, suit,
  1961-1962 .... 650.00
  Ballgown 800.00
  In trunk with wardrobe, 1962, 1966-1967 .... 1200.00 up
  In riding habit,1962.. 575.00
  In gown from cover of 1962 catalog... 700.00
  10" (25cm) hard plastic, 1962 .... 550.00
JAMAICA 8" (20cm) straight leg, 1986-1988 .... 75.00
JANIE 12" (31cm) toddler, 1964-1966 .... 285.00
  Ballerina, 1965 .... 250.00
  14" (36cm) baby, 1972-1973 .... 70.00
  20" (51cm) baby, 1972-1973 .... 90.00
JAPAN 8" (20cm) hard plastic, bend knee, 1968-1972 .... 95.00
  8" (20cm) hard plastic, straight leg, 1973-1975... 60.00
  8" (20cm) hard plastic, straight leg, 1976-1986... 55.00
  8" (20cm), 1987-1991 .... 55.00
  8" (20cm) hard plastic, white face, re-introduced 1992-1993, ... 60.00
JASMINE 10" (25cm), Portrette Series, 1987-1988 .... 75.00
JEANNIE WALKER 13-14" (33-36cm) composition, 1940s 400.00
  18" (46cm) composition, 1940s 500.00
JENNIFER'S TRUNK SET 14" (36cm) doll and wardrobe, 1990...................... 245.00
JESSICA 18" (46cm) cloth, vinyl, 1990... 145.00
JO (*see Little Women*)
JOANIE 36" (91cm) plastic,vinyl, 1960-1961 .... 450.00 up
  36" (91cm) Nurse, all white with black band on cap, 1960 .... 400.00 up
  36" (91cm) Nurse, colored dress, all white pinafore and cap, 1961 .... 385.00
JOHN 8" (20cm), Storyland Dolls, 1993... 45.00
JOHN POWER'S MODELS 14" (36cm) hard plastic, 1952 (mint) .... 1500.00 up
  18" (46cm) hard plastic, 1952 (mint) .... 1300.00 up
JONES, CASEY 8" (20cm) hard plastic, Americana Series, 1991 .... 52.00
JOSEPHINE 12" (31cm), Portraits of History, 1980-1986 .... 45.00
JOY 12" (31cm) porcelain, New England Collectors, 1990
  (*see Special Dolls*) 250.00
JOY NOEL TREE TOPPER 10" (25cm) hard plastic, made for Spiegel,
  1992 (*see Special Dolls*) 125.00

The Coronation of Queen Elizabeth II was the first such English event televised in the United States.
Madame Alexander made a *Coronation Series* of dolls that were on display during the Coronation in
1953. One-of-a-kind dolls, they were all hard plastic and today they reside at the Brooklyn Children's
Museum. Due to renovations, they are not on display. *Alexander Doll Company, Bob Gantz,
photographer.*

Judy   21" (53cm) hard plastic, vinyl arms, 1962 (catalog special) ....$ 1700.00
Jugo-slav   7" (18cm) composition, 1935-1937 ....265.00
Juliet   18" (46cm) composition, 1937-1940 ....1200.00
  21" (53cm) composition, Portrait Series, 1945-1946................................1900.00
  8" (20cm) hard plastic, 1955..800.00-900.00
  12" (31cm) plastic, vinyl, Portrait Children Series, 1978-1987....................45.00
  12" (31cm), Romance Collection, re-introduced 1991-1992 ....105.00
June Bride   21" (53cm) composition, Portrait Series, 1939,
  1946-1947, ... 1700.00-1900.00
June Wedding   8" (20cm) hard plastic, 1956...600.00

K   **Karen Ballerina**   15" (38cm) composition, 1947-1949 ....700.00
  18-21" (46-53cm)..750.00
  15-18" (38-46cm) hard plastic, 1948-1949 ....875.00
Kate Greenaway   16" (41cm) cloth, 1936-1938 ....900.00
  7" (18cm) composition, 1838-1943 ....350.00
  9" (23cm) composition, 1936-1939 ....375.00
  13" (33cm) composition, 1938-1943 ....600.00
  18" (46cm) composition, 1938-1943 ....700.00
  24" (61cm) compositon, 1938-1943 ....850.00
  14" (36cm), Classic Dolls, 1993 ....110.00
Kathleen Toddler   23" (58cm) rigid vinyl, 1959 ....125.00
Kathy   15-18" (38-46cm) hard plastic, has braids, 1949-1951 ....700.00-900.00
Kathy Baby   13-15" (33-38cm) vinyl, rooted or molded hair,
  1954-1956 ....65.00-125.00
  11" (28cm) vinyl, molded hair, with trousseau, 1955-1956 ....125.00
  11-13" (28-33cm) vinyl, rooted or molded hair, 1955-1956 ....65.00-125.00
  18-21" (46-53cm), rooted or molded hair, 1954-1956 ....100.00-150.00
  21" (53cm), 1954 ....165.00
  21" (53cm) and 25" (64cm), 1955-1956 ....125.00-200.00
Kathy Cry Dolly   11-15" (28-38cm) vinyl, 1957-1958 ....60.00-85.00
  18" (46cm), 21" (53cm), 25" (64cm) 75.00-125.00
Kathy Tears   11"(28cm), 15" (38cm), 17" (43cm) vinyl,
  closed mouth, 1959-1962 ....50.00-85.00
  19" (48cm), 23" (58cm), 26" (66cm), 1959-1962 ....100.00-150.00
  12" (31cm), 16" (41cm), 19" (48cm) vinyl, 1960-1961 ....60.00-85.00
Katie (Black Smarty)   12" (31cm) plastic, vinyl, 1963 ....350.00
Katie   12" (31cm) hard plastic, made for FAO Schwarz 100th
  Anniversary, 1962 ....1200.00
  12" (31cm), Black Janie, 1965 ....325.00
Keane, Doris   cloth, 1930s 800.00
  9-11" (23-28cm) composition, 1936-1937...285.00
Kelly   12" (31cm) hard plastic, 1959 ....425.00
  15-16" (38-41cm), 1958-1959 ....300.00
  16" (41cm) in trunk, wardrobe, 1959 ....485.00
  22" (56cm), 1958-1959 ....450.00
Kennedy, Jacqueline   14" (36cm), 6th set,
  First Ladies Series, 1989-1990..150.00
Kitten   24" (61cm), rooted hair, 1961 ....85.00
  14-18" (36-46cm) cloth, vinyl, 1962-1963 ....35.00-75.00
  20" (51cm), nurser, doesn't wet, cryer box, 1968 ....75.00
  20" (51cm), dressed in pink, 1985-1986 ....85.00
Kitten Kries   20" (51cm) cloth, vinyl, 1967 ....85.00
Kitten, Lively   14" (36cm), 18" (46cm), 24" (61cm), knob moves head
  and limbs, 1962-1963 ....100.00 up

Kitten, Mama   18" (46cm), same as "Lively" but also has cryer box, 1963 ....$ 100.00 up
Klondike Kate   10" (25cm) hard plastic, 1963 .... 1000.00
Korea   8" (20cm) hard plastic, bend knee, 1968-1970 ....200.00
Re-introduced 1988-1989 ....90.00

L

Lady & Child, Her   21" (53cm) porcelain, and 8" (20cm) hard plastic, 1993 ....500.00
Lady Bird   8" (20cm), Storyland Dolls, 1988-1989 ....90.00
Lady Hamilton   11" (28cm) hard plastic, pink silk gown, picture hat, 1957 ....425.00
20" (51cm) hard plastic, vinyl arms, picture hat, blue gown with shoulder shawl effect, Models Formal Series, 1957 ....750.00
21" (53cm), #2182, beige lace over pink gown, 1968 ....475.00
12" (31cm) vinyl, Portraits of History, 1984-1986 ....55.00
Lady in Red   21" (53cm), red taffeta, 1958 ....1500.00
10" (25cm), Portrette Series, 1990 ....75.00
Lady in Waiting   8" (20cm) hard plastic, 1955..1200.00
Lady Lee   8" (20cm), Storyland Dolls, 1988 ....90.00
Lady Lovelace   cloth, felt, 1930s 600.00
Lady Windermere   21" (53cm) composition, 1945-1946 ....1800.00
Lane, Harriet   3rd set, First Ladies Series, 1982-1984 ....95.00
Laos   8" (20cm) straight leg, 1987-1988 ....75.00

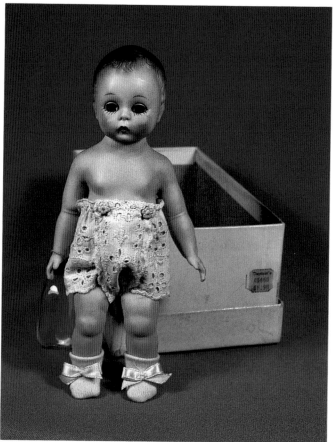

A very rare and unusual 8in (20cm) infant doll in a Dayton's Department Store box. The head is hard plastic, and the body is all one-piece stuffed vinyl.

LAPLAND 8" (20cm), International Dolls, 1993	$ 50.00
LATVIA 8" (20cm) straight leg, 1987	75.00
LAUGHING ALLEGRA cloth, 1932	700.00
LAURIE, LITTLE MEN 8" (20cm) hard plastic, bend knee, 1966-1972	135.00
Check pants	55.00
Straight leg, 1973-1975	60.00
Straight leg, 1976-1992	50.00
12" (31cm) all hard plastic, 1966 only	450.00
12" (31cm) plastic, vinyl, 1967-1988	75.00
12" (31cm) plastic, vinyl, made for Sears, 1989-1990 (*see Little Women*)	
LAZY MARY 7" (18cm) composition, 1936-1938	275.00
LE PETIT BOUDOIR 10" (25cm), Collector's United, 1992	
(*see Special Dolls*)	135.00
LENA (*see River Boat*)	
LENNOX, MARY 14" (36cm), Classic Dolls, 1993	100.00
LESLIE (BLACK POLLY) 17" (43cm) vinyl, in dress, 1965-1971	375.00
Ballerina, 1966-1971	350.00
Bride, 1966-1971	300.00
In formal, 1965-1971	465.00
In trunk, wardrobe	700.00 up
LETTY BRIDESMAID 7-8" (18-20cm) composition, 1938-1940	275.00
LEWIS, SHARI 14" (36cm), 1958-1959	750.00
21" (53cm), 1958-1959	950.00

Margot was the racy friend of *Cissette*. Her glamorous good looks belie the fact she was made from the same molds. To date, all 10in (25cm) dolls are made from the molds first developed in 1957.

LIESL (*see Sound of Music*)
'LIL CHRISTMAS COOKIE 8" (20cm), Americana Series, 1993 .... $ 55.00
'LIL CLARA & NUTCRACKER 8" (20cm), 1993 .... 50.00
'LIL MISS GENIUS 7" (18cm) vinyl, 1993 .... 40.00
'LIL SIR GENIUS 7" (18cm), 1993 .... 40.00
LILA BRIDESMAID 7-8" (18-20cm) composition, 1938-1940 .... 265.00
LILAC FAIRIE BALLERINA 21"(53cm) plastic, vinyl, Portrait, 1993 .... 300.00
LILIBET 16" (41cm) composition, 1938 .... 750.00
LILY 10" (25cm) hard plastic, 1987-1988 .... 75.00
LINCOLN, MARY TODD 3rd set, First Ladies Series, 1982-1984 .... 150.00
LIND, JENNY 10" (25cm), all pink, no trim, Portrette Series, 1969 .... 650.00
   10" (25cm) hard plastic, pink with lace trim, Portrette Series, 1970 .... 650.00
   14" (36cm) plastic, vinyl, Portrait Children Series, 1970-1971 .... 385.00
   21" (53cm) hard plastic, vinyl arms, dressed in all pink, no trim, 1969 .... 1200.00
   21" (53cm) plastic, vinyl, all pink with lace trim, 1970 .... 1300.00
LIND, JENNY & LISTENING CAT 14" (36cm) plastic, vinyl, Portrait
   Children Series, 1970-1971 .... 385.00
LION TAMER 8" (20cm), Americana Series, 1990 .... 80.00
LISSY 11½-12" (29-31cm) hard plastic, jointed knees and elbows,
   1956-1958 .... 285.00
   Ballerina, 1956 and 1958 .... 325.00
   Bride, 1956-1958 (*see Lissy under Bride*) 300.00
   Bridesmaid, 1956-1957 .... 400.00
   Street dresses, 1956-1958 .... 285.00
   Window box with wardrobe, 1956 .... 1500.00
   21" (53cm), Portrait, pink tiara, 1966 .... 1950.00
LITTLE ANGEL 9" (23cm) latex, vinyl, 1950-1957 .... 175.00
LITTLE BETTY 9-11" (23-28cm) composition, 1935-1943 .... 265.00
LITTLE BITSEY 9" (23cm), vinyl, nurser, 1967-1968 .... 165.00
LITTLE BO PEEP (*see Bo Peep, Little*)
LITTLE BOY BLUE 7" (18cm) composition, 1937-1939 .... 275.00 up
LITTLE BUTCH 9" (23cm) all vinyl nurser, 1967-1968 .... 165.00
LITTLE CHERUB 11" (28cm) composition, 1945-1946 .... 365.00
   7" (18cm) all vinyl, 1960 .... 275.00
LITTLE COLONEL 8½-9" (22-23cm) composition, closed mouth,
   (rare size), 1935 .... 750.00
   11-13" (28-33cm) composition, closed mouth 575.00-650.00
   14-17" (36-43cm), composition, open mouth 650.00-675.00
   18-23" (46-58cm), composition, open mouth 775.00-850.00
   26-27" (66-69cm), composition, open mouth 1000.00
LITTLE DEVIL 8" (20cm) hard plastic, Americana Series, 1992-1993 .... 55.00
LITTLE DORRIT 16" (41cm) cloth, Dicken's character, early 1930s 700.00
LITTLE EMILY 16" (41cm) cloth, Dicken's character, early 1930s 700.00
LITTLE EMPEROR 8" (20cm), UFDC luncheon, 1992 (*see Special Dolls*) 600.00
LITTLE GENIUS 12-14" (31-36cm) composition, cloth, 1935-1940,
   1942-1946 .... 125.00
   18-20" (46-51cm) composition, cloth, 1935-1937, 1942-1946 .... 145.00-165.00
   24-25" (61-64cm) composition, cloth, 1936-1940 .... 165.00-185.00
   8" (20cm) hard plastic, vinyl, undressed, 1956-1962 .... 125.00
      Christening outfit 350.00
      Cotton play dress 225.00
      Dressy, lacy outfit with bonnet 275.00
LITTLE GODEY 8" (20cm) hard plastic, 1953-1955 .... 950.00 up
LITTLE GRANNY 14" (36cm) plastic, vinyl, 1966 .... 225.00
   14" (36cm), pinstripe or floral gown, 1966 .... 225.00

LITTLE HUGGUMS   12" (31cm), made for I. Magnin, 1992
(*see Special Dolls*) ....$ 95.00
christening dress,   12" (31cm), 1993 ....55.00
Denton,   12" (31cm), 1993 ....40.00
dress,   12" (31cm), 1993 ....42.00
pajamas,   12" (31cm), 1993 ....42.00
pink check with hat,   1993 ....50.00
pink teatime,   12" (31cm), 1993 ....47.00
sailor suit,   12" (31cm), 1993 ....45.00
LITTLE JACK HORNER   7" (18cm) composition, 1937-1943 ....325.00
LITTLE JUMPING JOAN   8" (20cm), Storyland Dolls, 1989-1990 ....90.00
LITTLE LADY DOLL   8" (20cm) hard plastic, gift set, mint, 1960 ....1200.00
8" (20cm) doll 325.00
21" (53cm) hard plastic, has braids and Colonial gown, 1949 ....2000.00
LITTLE LORD FAUNTLEROY   16" (41cm) cloth, 1930s 700.00
13" (33cm) composition, 1936-1937 ....685.00
LITTLE MADELINE   8" (20cm) hard plastic, in pink or blue, 1953 ....625.00
LITTLE MAID   8" (20cm) straight leg, Storyland Dolls, 1987-1988................90.00
LITTLE MELANIE   8" (20cm) hard plastic, 1955-1956 ....950.00 up
LITTLE MEN (NAT, STUFFY AND TOMMY BANGS)   15" (38cm)
hard plastic, circa 1950 ....800.00 each, 2400.00 set
LITTLE MERMAID   10" (25cm) hard plastic, Portrette Series, 1992-1993 ....105.00
LITTLE MINISTER   8" (20cm) hard plastic, 1957 ....1500.00 up
LITTLE MISS   8" (20cm) hard plastic, Storyland Dolls, 1989-1991 ....55.00
LITTLE MISS GODEY   8" (20cm) hard plastic, MADC, 1992 (*see Special Dolls*) ....S/A
LITTE MISS MAGNIN   8" (20cm) hard plastic, I. MAGNIN, 1991-1992
(*see Special Dolls*) 80.00
LITTLE MISS MUFFET   8" (20cm) hard plastic, Storyland, 1993 ....60.00
LITTLE NANNIE ETTICOAT   straight leg, Storyland Dolls, 1986-1988 ....90.00
LITTLE NELL   16" (41cm) cloth, Dickens character, early 1930s 700.00
14" (36cm) composition, 1938-1940 ....650.00
LITTLE SHAVER   7" (18cm) cloth, 1940-1944 ....485.00
10" (25cm) cloth, 1940-1944 ....475.00
15" (38cm) cloth, 1940-1944 ....525.00
22" (56cm), cloth, 1940-1944 ....550.00
12" (31cm) plastic, vinyl, painted eyes, 1963-1965 ....300.00
LITTLE SOUTHERN BOY/GIRL   10" (25cm) latex, vinyl, 1950-1951 ....150.00 each
LITTLE SOUTHERN GIRL   8" (20cm) hard plastic, 1953 ....975.00
LITTLE VICTORIA   7½-8" (19-20cm), 1953-1954 ....1300.00
LITTLE WOMEN   (Meg, Jo, Amy, Beth, later Marme or Marmee)
16" (41cm) cloth, 1930-1936 ....600.00
7" (18cm) composition, 1935-1944 ....275.00 each
9" (23cm) composition, 1937-1940 ....295.00 each
14-15" (36-38cm) hard plastic, 1947-1950 ....425.00 each
14-15" (36-38cm), *Amy* with loop curls, 1947-1950 ....475.00
14-15" (36-38cm) hard plastic, spread fingers, early 1950s ....375.00 each
matched set ....675.00 each
11½-12" (29-31cm) hard plastic, jointed elbows and knees, 1957-1958.....300.00 each
11½-12" (29-31cm) hard plastic, one-piece arms and legs, 1959-1966 ......225.00 each
7½-8" (19-20cm) hard plastic, straight leg walker, plus "Marme", 1955....285.00 each
8" (20cm) hard plastic, bend knee walker, 1956-1959 ....200.00 each
8" (20cm) bend knee, 1960-1972 ....135.00 each
8" (20cm) straight leg, 1973-1975 ....60.00 each
8" (20cm) straight leg, 1976-1992 ....50.00 each

12" (31cm) plastic, vinyl, 1969-1982 .... $ 65.00 each
12" (31cm) plastic, vinyl, new outfits, 1983-1989 .... 65.00 each
12" (31cm) set made for Sears, 1989-1990 (*see Special Dolls*) 475.00
12" (31cm) hard plastic, 1993 .... 100.00
LITTLEST KITTEN   8" (20cm) vinyl, nude, 1963 .... 175.00
  Christening outfit 325.00
  Dressy, lacy outfit and bonnet 275.00
  Play outfits 150.00
LIVELY HUGGUMS   25" (64cm), knob moves limbs and makes head
  move, 1963 .... 100.00
LIVELY KITTEN   14" (36cm), 18" (46cm), 24" (61cm), knob moves
  limbs and makes head turn, 1962-1963 .... 145.00
LIVELY PUSSY CAT   14" (36cm), 20" (51cm), 24" (61cm), knob moves
  limbs and makes head move, 1966-1969 .... 100.00
LOLA AND LOLLIE BRIDESMAID   7" (18cm) composition, 1938-1940 .... 350.00 each
LOLLIE BABY   rubber, composition, 1941-1942 .... 95.00
LORD FAUNTLEROY   12" (31cm), Portrait Children, 1981-1983 .... 70.00
LOUISA   (*see Sound of Music*)
LOVEY DOVEY   19" (48cm) vinyl baby, closed mouth, molded or
  rooted hair, 1958-1959 .... 165.00

An 8in (20cm) *Scotts Lass* has the smiling face first utilized on the *Maggie Mix-Up* doll in 1960-61. Still used today, collectors refer to this as the smile face.

12" (31cm) all hard plastic toddler, 1948-1951 .... $ 350.00
19" (48cm) hard plastic, latex, 1950-1951 .... 195.00
LUCINDA   12" (31cm) plastic, vinyl, 1969-1970 .... 345.00
   14" (36cm) plastic, vinyl, blue gown, 1971-1982 .... 90.00
   14" (36cm), pink or peach gown, Classic Dolls, 1983-1986 .... 75.00
LUCK OF THE IRISH   8" (20cm), Americana Series, 1992-1993 .... 55.00
LUCY   8" (20cm) hard plastic, Americana Series, 1961 .... 1200.00 up
LUCY BRIDE   14" (36cm) composition, 1937-1940 .... 375.00
   17" (43cm) composition, 1937-1940 .... 475.00
   14" (36cm) hard plastic, 1949-1950 .... 500.00 up
   17" (43cm) hard plastic, 1949-1950 .... 550.00
LUCY LOCKET   8" (20cm) straight leg, Storyland Dolls, 1986-1988 .... 75.00

M MADAME (ALEXANDER)   21" (53cm), one-piece skirt in pink, 1984 .... 400.00
   21" (53cm), pink with overskirt, 1985-1987 .... 375.00
   21" (53cm), blue with full lace overskirt, 1988-1990 .... 345.00
MADAME BUTTERFLY   10" (25cm), made for Marshall Fields, 1990
   (see Special Dolls) 90.00
MADAME DOLL   21" (53cm) hard plastic, vinyl arms, pink brocade,
   1966 only 2300.00
   14" (36cm) plastic, vinyl, Classic Dolls, 1967-1975 .... 200.00 up
MADAME POMPADOUR   21" (53cm) hard plastic, vinyl arms, pink
   lace overskirt, 1970 .... 1200.00

An unusual 8in (20cm) all hard plastic *Maggie Mix-up* from the early 1960s is this pouty mouth version using the *Wendy* doll molds. Collectors specializing in 8in (20cm) dolls are always looking for variations.

MADELAINE   14" (36cm) composition, 1940-1942 ....$ 550.00
    8" (20cm) hard plastic, FAO Schwarz special, 1954 ....750.00
    17-18" (43-46cm) hard plastic, 1949-1952 ....700.00
MADELAINE DU BAIN   11" (28cm) composition, closed mouth, 1937 ....450.00
    14" (36cm) composition, 1938-1939 ....475.00
    17" (43cm) composition, 1939-1941 ....575.00
    21" (53cm) composition, 1939-1941 ....775.00
    14" (36cm) hard plastic, 1949-1951 ....950.00
MADELINE   17-18" (43-46cm) hard plastic, jointed elbows and knees,
    1950-1953 ....550.00
    18" (46cm) hard plastic, vinyl head, jointed body, 1961 ....795.00
MADISON, DOLLY   1st set, First Ladies Series, 1976-1978 ....120.00
MAGGIE   15" (38cm) hard plastic, 1948-1952 ....450.00
    17-18" (43-46cm) hard plastic, 1949-1952 ....625.00
    20-21" (51-53cm) hard plastic, 1948-1952 ....650.00
    22-23" (56-58cm) hard plastic, 1949-1952 ....750.00
    17" (43cm) plastic, vinyl, 1972-1973 ....175.00
MAGGIE MIXUP
    8" (20cm) hard plastic, 1960-1961 ....425.00
    8" (20cm) in riding habit, 1960-1961 ....550.00
    8" (20cm) in skater outfit, 1960-1961 ....550.00
    8" (20cm) hard plastic, Angel, 1961 ....675.00

A proud Madame Alexander stands in front of a display cabinet in the New York showroom in 1965.

8" (20cm) in overalls, watering can, 1961 .... $ 650.00
17" (43cm) plastic, vinyl, 1960-1961 .... 375.00
MAGGIE TEENAGER   15-18" (38-46cm) hard plastic, 1951-1952 .... 500.00
23" (58cm), 1951-1953 .... 650.00
MAGGIE WALKER   15-18" (38-46cm) hard plastic, 1949-1952 .... 400.00
20-21" (51-53cm), 1949-1952 .... 550.00
23-25" (58-64cm), 1951-1952 .... 600.00
MAGNOLIA   21" (53cm), rows of lace on pink gown, 1977 .... 500.00
21" (53cm), yellow gown, 1988 .... 275.00
MAID MARIAN   8" (20cm) hard plastic, Storyland Dolls, 1989-1991 .... 60.00
21" (53cm), Portrait Series, 1993 .... 300.00
MAID OF HONOR   18" (46cm) composition, 1940-1944 .... 700.00
14" (36cm) plastic, vinyl, Classic Dolls, 1988-1989 .... 85.00
MAJORETTE   14-17" (36-43cm) composition, 1937-1938 .... 850.00
8" (20cm) hard plastic, 1955 .... 700.00
8" (20cm), Americana Series, 1991-1992 .... 55.00
MAMMY   8" (20cm), Jubilee II set, 1989 .... 90.00
8" (20cm) hard plastic, Scarlett Series, 1991-1992 .... 55.00
MANET   21" (53cm), light brown with dark brown pinstripes, 1982-1983 ..... 200.00
14" (36cm), Fine Arts Series, 1986-1987 .... 75.00
MARCH HARE   cloth, felt, mid 1930s 700.00
MARGARET ROSE   (see Princess)
MARGOT   10" (25cm) hard plastic, formals, 1961 .... 450.00
Street dresses, bathing suit, 1961 .... 300.00
MARGOT BALLERINA   15-18" (38-46cm), 1953-1955 .... 450.00
15-18" (38-46cm) hard plastic, vinyl arms, 1955 .... 325.00
MARIA   (see Sound of Music)
MARIE ANTOINETTE   21" (53cm) composition, Portrait, 1940s 1500.00
21" (53cm), floral print with pink insert, 1987-1988 .... 285.00
MARINE (BOY)   14" (36cm) composition, 1943-1944 .... 750.00
MARIONETTES, TONY SARG   composition, 1934-1940 .... 265.00
12" (31cm) composition, made for Disney® 325.00
MARME   (see Little Women)
MARTA   (see Sound of Music)
MARTI GRAS   10" (25cm), made for Spiegel, 1992 (see Special Dolls) 135.00
MARTIN, MARY   14-17" (36-43cm) hard plastic, formal,
1948-1951 .... 750.00-900.00
14-17" (36-43cm), in sailor suit, 1948-1951 .... 850.00-1000.00
MARY ANN   14" (36cm) plastic, vinyl, ballerina, 1965 .... 225.00
Assorted outfits 200.00
MARYBEL   16" (41cm) rigid vinyl, The Doll Who Gets Well, 1959-1965
In case, 1959, 1961, 1965 .... 350.00
In case with wardrobe, 1960 .... 375.00
In case, with long, straight hair, 1965 .... 400.00
MARY CASSATT BABY   14" (36cm) cloth, vinyl, 1969-1970 .... 150.00
14" (36cm) plastic, vinyl child, Fine Arts Series, 1987 .... 75.00
20" (51cm), 1969-1970 .... 225.00
MARY ELLEN   31" (79cm) hard plastic, 1954 .... 600.00
31" (79cm) plastic, vinyl arms, jointed elbows, 1955 .... 450.00
MARY ELLEN PLAYMATE   14" (36cm) plastic, vinyl, Marshall Fields
exclusive, 1965 .... 300.00
12" (31cm) in case with wigs, 1965 .... 675.00
MARY GRAY   14" (36cm) plastic, vinyl, Classic Dolls, 1988 .... 75.00

MARY LOUISE
    8" (20cm) hard plastic, same as 18" (46cm), Me and My Shadow
       Series, 1954 ....$ 950.00 up
    18" (46cm) hard plastic, orange and green, Me and My Shadow
       Series, 1954 .... 1200.00
MARY, MARY   8" (20cm) hard plastic, bend knee,
Storyland Dolls, 1965-1972 .... 135.00
    8" (20cm) hard plastic, straight leg, 1973-1975 .... 60.00
    8" (20cm) hard plastic, straight leg, 1976-1987 .... 55.00
    8" (20cm), hard plastic, re-introduced 1992 .... 55.00
    14" (36cm), plastic/vinyl, Classic Dolls, 1988-1991 .... 75.00
MARY MINE   21" (53cm) cloth, vinyl, 1977-1989 .... 125.00
    14" (36cm) cloth, vinyl, 1977-1979 .... 75.00
    14" (36cm), re-introduced 1989 .... 60.00
MARY MUSLIN   19" (48cm) cloth, 1951 .... 650.00
    26" (66cm), 1951 .... 750.00
    40" (101cm), 1951 .... 950.00
MARY, QUEEN OF SCOTS   21" (53cm), 1988-1989 .... 350.00
MARY ROSE BRIDE   17" (43cm) hard plastic, 1951 .... 575.00 up
MARY SUNSHINE   15" (38cm) plastic, vinyl, 1961 .... 365.00
MCELROY, MARY   4th set, First Ladies Series, 1985-1987 .... 90.00

Using the mold first used on *Cissette* in 1957, this early 1960s *Gibson Girl* has deeper and richer make-up with a French Twist hairstyle.

McGUFFEY ANA   16" (41cm) cloth, 1934-1936 .... $ 650.00
   7" (18cm) composition, 1935-1939 .... 325.00
   9" (23cm) composition, 1935-1939 .... 375.00
   11" (28cm) closed mouth, 1937-1939 .... 600.00
   11-13" (28-33cm) composition, 1937-1944 .... 500.00-600.00
   13" (33cm) composition, 1938 .... 675.00
   14-16" (36-41cm) composition, 1937-1944 .... 500.00-600.00
   14½" (37cm) composition, coat, hat and muff, 1948 .... 700.00
   15" (38cm) composition, 1935-1937 .... 600.00
   17" (43cm) composition, 1948-1949 .... 775.00
   17-20" (43-51cm) composition, 1937-1943 .... 685.00-800.00
   21-25" (53-64cm) composition, 1937-1942 .... 750.00-900.00
   28" (71cm) composition, 1937-1939 .... 985.00
   8" (20cm) hard plastic, 1956 .... 625.00
   18" (46cm), 25" (64cm), 31" (79cm), flat feet, 1955-1956 .... 485.00-800.00
   21" (53cm) hard plastic, 1948-1950 .... 850.00
   8" (20cm) hard plastic, was "American Girl" in 1962-1963, 1964-1965 .... 385.00
   14" (36cm) plastic, vinyl, plaid dress, eyelet apron, Classic Dolls,
     1968-1969 .... 125.00
   14" (36cm) plastic, vinyl, plaid dress, Classic Dolls, 1977-1986 .... 75.00
   14" (36cm) plastic, vinyl, mauve stripe pinafore, Classic Dolls,
     1987-1988 .... 70.00

The 8in (20cm) doll line had captivated the hearts of everyone by the early 1960s as shown in this twin set of *Wendy* and *Bill*.

8" (20cm), Storyland Dolls, 1990-1991 .... $ 55.00
12" (31cm) hard plastic, very rare doll, 1963 .... 1200.00 up
MᴄKᴇᴇ, Mᴀʀʏ   4th set, First Ladies Series, 1985-1987 .... 90.00
MᴄKɪɴʟᴇʏ, Iᴅᴀ   5th set, First Ladies Series, 1988.. 85.00
Mᴇᴅɪᴄɪ, Cᴀᴛʜᴇʀɪɴᴇ Dᴇ   21" (53cm) porcelain, 1990-1991 .... 525.00
Mᴇɢ (*see Little Women*)
Mᴇʟᴀɴɪᴇ
8" (20cm) hard plastic, 1955-1956 .... 1000.00
21" (53cm) hard plastic, vinyl arms, lace bodice and overdress
  over satin, 1961 .... 695.00
21" (53cm), blue gown, wide lace down sides, 1966................................ 2300.00
10" (25cm), pink multi-tiered skirt, 1969 .... 425.00
10" (25cm), yellow multi-tiered skirt, 1970 .... 425.00
21" (53cm), blue, white rick-rack around hem ruffle, blonde, 1967 .... 575.00
21" (53cm), rust faille gown, braid trim, brown velvet hat, 1968 .... 550.00
21" (53cm), blue gown, white trim, multi-rows of lace, bonnet, 1969 .... 500.00
21" (53cm), white gown, red ribbon trim, 1970 .... 550.00
21" (53cm), blue gown, white sequin trim, 1971 .... 450.00
21" (53cm), white gown, red jacket and bonnet, 1974 .... 500.00
21" (53cm), white nylon gown with pink trim, 1979, 1980........................ 350.00

As the 1960s raced on, little girls were dreaming of the future. The *Wendy* line reflected, however, the child in the present, as shown in this A-line dress on a mint doll.

21" (53cm), pink nylon with blue ribbon, 1981 .... $ 300.00
12" (31cm), green gown, brown trim, Portrait Children Series, 1987 .... 95.00
10" (25cm), all royal blue, black trim, Jubilee II, 1989 .... 85.00
8" (20cm), lavender, lace, Scarlett Series, 1990 .... 65.00
8" (20cm), peach gown, bonnet with lace, 1992 .... 57.00
21" (53cm), all orange with lace shawl, 1989 .... 300.00
MELINDA   10" (25cm) hard plastic, blue gown with white trim, 1968 .... 350.00
10" (25cm), yellow multi-tiered lace skirt, 1970 .... 350.00
14" (36cm), 16" (41cm), 22" (56cm) plastic, vinyl, 1963 .... 250.00-425.00 up
14" (36cm) ballerina, 1963 .... 325.00
16-22" (41-56cm) plastic, vinyl, 1962-1963 .... 365.00
MELODY AND FRIEND   8" (20cm) hard plastic, Alexander and 26" (66cm)
porcelain, Gunzel, 1991 (*see Special Dolls*) 850.00
MERRY ANGEL   8" (20cm), made for Spiegel, 1991 (*see Special Dolls*) 185.00
MEXICO   7" (18cm) composition, 1936 .... 265.00
9" (23cm) composition, 1938-1939 .... 285.00
8" (20cm) hard plastic, bend knee walker, 1964-1965 .... 150.00
8" (20cm) hard plastic, bend knee, 1965-1972 .... 125.00
8" (20cm) straight leg, 1973-1975 .... 60.00
8" (20cm) straight leg, 1976-1991 .... 45.00

Called a jewel in the crown of the Alexander Doll
Company, this mold for a 21in (53cm) doll was
used on the Portrait dolls of 1966 and a doll named
Coco.

MICHAEL   11" (28cm) plastic, vinyl, with teddy bear, 1969 (Peter Pan set) ..$ 350.00
    8" (20cm), Storyland Dolls, 1992-1993 ....52.00
MIDNIGHT   21" (53cm), dark blue, black, 1990 ....250.00
MIMI   30" (76cm), multi-jointed body, in formal, 1961 ....800.00
    Red sweater, plaid skirt 450.00
    Romper suit, skirt 450.00
    Slacks, stripe top, straw hat..450.00
    Tyrolean outfit 900.00
    14" (36cm), Opera Series, 1983-1986 ....90.00
    21" (53cm) hard plastic, vinyl arms, pink cape and trim on white
        gown, Portrait Series, 1971 ....525.00
MISS AMERICA   14" (36cm) composition, 1941-1943 ....750.00
MISS LEIGH   8" (20cm), CU Gathering, 1989 (see Special Dolls) ....250.00 up
MISS LIBERTY   10" (25cm), MADC, 1991 (see Special Dolls)........................125.00
MISS MAGNIN   10" (25cm), made for I. Magnin, 1991 (see Special Dolls)....125.00
MISS MUFFETT   8" (20cm) hard plastic, bend knee, Storyland Dolls,
    1965-1972 .... 125.00
    8" (20cm) straight leg, 1973-1975 ....60.00
    8" (20cm) straight leg, 1976-1986 ....55.00
    8" (20cm) straight leg, 1987-1988 ....65.00

A 10in (25cm) *Renoir* and an 8in (20cm) *Red Boy* from the late 1960s and 1970s, respectively, showed that the Classical influence was still part of the Madame Alexander tradition.

Miss Scarlett   14" (36cm) plastic/vinyl, made for Belk & Leggett, 1988
(*see Special Dolls*) ....$ 100.00
Miss Unity   10" (25cm) hard plastic, UFDC, 1991 (*see Special Dolls*) 250.00
Miss U.S.A.   8" (20cm) hard plastic, bend knee, Americana Series,
1966-1968 ....300.00
Miss Victory   20" (51cm) composition, magnetic hands, 1944-1946 ....750.00
Mistress Mary   7" (18cm) composition, 1937-1941 ....265.00
Molly   14" (36cm), Classic Dolls, 1988 ....75.00
Molly Cottontail   cloth, felt, 1930s 600.00
Mombo   8" (20cm) hard plastic, *Wendy Loves the Mombo*, 1955 ....650.00
Mommy and Me   14" (36cm) and 9" (23cm) composition,
matching outfits, 1940-1943 .... 1500.00 set
Mommy's Pet   14-20" (36-51cm) cloth, vinyl, 1977-1986 ....40.00-60.00
Monet   21" (53cm) hard plastic, black and white check gown with
red jacket, 1984-1985..285.00
Monique   8" (20cm) hard plastic, Disneyland® Teddy Bear & Classic
Dolls, 1993 (*see Special Dolls*)...595.00
Monroe, Elizabeth   lst set, First Ladies Series, 1976-1978 ....120.00
Morisot   21" (53cm) plastic, vinyl, lime green gown with white lace, 1985-1986 .225.00
Morocco   8" (20cm) hard plastic, bend knee, 1968-1970 ....350.00

Fondly called, *Easter Doll*, this late 1960s doll was made in an edition of under 350 pieces by request from Frank Martin, an Alexander Doll Company sales representative. The doll, like Frank Martin, is still a favorite with collectors!

Moss Rose   14" (36cm), Classic Dolls, 1991 ....$ 155.00
Mother Goose   8" (20cm) straight leg, Storyland Dolls, 1986-1993 ....55.00
Mother Hubbard   8" (20cm), Storyland Dolls, 1988-1989 ....60.00
Mouseketeer   8" (20cm), made for Disney®, 1991 (see Special Dolls) 95.00
Mr. O'Hara   8" (20cm), Scarlett Series, 1993 ....53.00
Mrs. Buck Rabbit   cloth, felt, mid-1930s 600.00
Mrs. March Hare   cloth, felt, mid-1930s 600.00
Mrs. O'Hara   8" (20cm), Scarlett Series, 1992-1993 ....57.00
Mrs. Quack-A-Field   cloth, felt, mid-1930s 650.00
Mrs. Snoopie   cloth, felt, 1940s 650.00
Muffin   19" (48cm) cloth, 1966 ....100.00
    14" (36cm), 1963-1977 ....100.00
    12" (31cm) all vinyl, 1989-1990 ....60.00
    12" (31cm), in trunk, wardrobe, 1990-1991 ....150.00
My Little Sweetheart   white and black, made for A Child at Heart,
    1992 (see Special Dolls) ....95.00 up

N Nan McDare   Cloth, felt, 1940s 650.00
Nana Governess   8" (20cm) hard plastic, 1957.............................1200.00 up
Nana Storyland   (stuffed dog),, 1993 ....40.00

12in (31cm) *Suzy* is an adorable pigeon toed toddler whose face was used for *Janie, Frederick, Rozy,* and a recent reissue named *Muffin.*

Nancy Dawson   8" (20cm) hard plastic, Storyland Dolls, 1988-1989 .... $ 90.00
Nancy Drew   12" (31cm) plastic, vinyl, Literature Series, 1967 .... 375.00
Nancy Jean   8" (20cm) hard plastic, made for Belk & Leggett, 1990
   (*see Special Dolls*) 75.00
Napoleon   12" (31cm) plastic, vinyl, Portraits of History, 1980-1986 .... 60.00
Natasha   21" (53cm), brown and paisley brocade, 1989-1990 .... 345.00
National Velvet   12" (31cm) plastic, vinyl, Romance Series, 1991 .... 80.00
Neiman Marcus   8" (20cm) hard plastic, party trunk, 1990
   (*see Special Dolls*) 275.00
Nelson, Lord   12" (31cm) plastic, vinyl, Portraits of History, 1984-1986 ..... 65.00
Netherland Boy   Formerly "Dutch".
   8" (20cm) hard plastic, straight leg, 1974-1975 .... 65.00
   8" (20cm) hard plastic, straight leg, 1976-1989 .... 55.00
Netherland Girl   8" (20cm) hard plastic, 1974-1992 .... 55.00
Nicole   10" (25cm) hard plastic, Portrette Series, 1989-1990 .... 70.00
Nightingale, Florence   14" (36cm), Classic Dolls, 1986-1987 .... 60.00
Nina Ballerina   7" (18cm) composition, 1940 .... 285.00
   9" (23cm) composition, 1939-1941 .... 325.00
   14" (36cm) hard plastic, 1949-1950 .... 500.00
   15" (38cm) hard plastic, 1951 .... 600.00
   17" (43cm) hard plastic, 1949-1950 .... 500.00
   19" (48cm) hard plastic, 1949-1950 .... 650.00
   23" (58cm) hard plastic, 1951 .... 750.00

This 8in (20cm) *Alice in Wonderland* was a Disney® exclusive in the 1970s. Her white rabbit is also a Disney product.

NOEL   12" (31cm) porcelain, New England Collectors Society,
1989-1991 (*see Special Dolls*) ....$ 200.00 up
NORMANDY   7" (18cm) composition, 1935-1938 ....265.00
NORWAY   8" (20cm) hard plastic, bend knee, 1968-1972 ....135.00
   8" (20cm) straight leg, 1973-1975 ....60.00
   8" (20cm) straight leg, 1976-1987 ....55.00
NORWEGIAN   7-8" (18-20cm) composition, 1936-1940 ....265.00
   9" (23cm) composition, 1938-1939 ....285.00
NURSE   7" (18cm) composition, 1936-1939 ....285.00
   13" (33cm) composition, Dionne nurse, 1936 ....500.00 up
   8" (20cm) hard plastic, all white, no baby, bend knee walker,
   1956-1957 ....500.00
   8" (20cm) with baby, stripe dress and pinafore, bend knee walker,
   1961-1965 ....450.00
   8" (20cm) hard plastic, blue, white striped dress, white pinafore and
   cap, Americana Series, 1990 ....60.00
   8" (20cm) hard plastic, white uniform, Americana Series, 1991 ....60.00
(*see Red Cross Nurse for additional listings*)

Always a heroine, *Snow White*, in 8in (20cm) size dressed in colors exclusive to the Disney® classic movie, was sold in the 1970s at the two theme parks.

O'BRIEN, MARGARET 14½" (37cm) composition, 1946-1947 ....$ 700.00
    18" (46cm), 21" (53cm) composition, 1946-1947 .... 850.00-975.00
    21-24" (53-61cm) composition, 1946-1947 .... 950.00-1200.00
    14½" (37cm) hard plastic, 1948-1951 .... 875.00 up
    18" (46cm) hard plastic, 1948-1951 .... 1000.00 up
    22" (56cm) hard plastic, 1948-1951 (very rare) .... 1250.00 up
OKTOBERFEST 8" (20cm), Greenville Show, 1992 (*see Special Dolls*) 150.00
OKTOBERFEST (BOY) 8" (20cm), Greenville Show, 1992
    (*see Special Dolls*) 150.00
OLD FASHIONED GIRL 13" (33cm) composition, 1945-1947 .... 425.00
    14" (36cm) hard plastic, 1948 .... 650.00
    20" (51cm) hard plastic, 1948 .... 700.00
OLIVER TWIST 16" (41cm) cloth, Dicken's character, 1934 .... 625.00
    7" (18cm) composition, 1935-1936 .... 285.00
    8" (20cm), Storyland Dolls, 1992 .... 50.00
OLIVER TWISTAIL cloth, felt, 1930s 700.00
OPENING NIGHT 10" (25cm), Portrette, 1989 .... 75.00
OPHELIA 12" (31cm), Romance Collection, 1992-1993 .... 115.00

The first Madame Alexander Fan Club Convention in 1983 featured this *Fairy God-mother* costume. It was not an Alexander Doll Company manufactured outfit but was designed by Judy La Manna. As the first convention souvenir costume, it is highly collectible today, despite not being an Alexander Doll Company design.

ORPHANT ANNIE   14" (36cm) plastic, vinyl, Literature Series, 1965-1966 .$ 325.00
1965 gift set...450.00 up

P PAKISTAN   8" (20cm) hard plastic, International Dolls, 1993 ....50.00
PAMELA   12" (31cm) hard plastic, with wigs, window box, 1963 ......475.00 up
In case, 1962-1963 ....900.00 up
12" vinyl head editions, in case, late 1960s ....500.00 up
PAMELA PLAYS DRESS UP AT GRANDMA'S   12" (31cm), hard plastic,
made for Horchow, 1993 (see Special Dolls) 250.00
PAN AMERICAN-POLLERA   7" (18cm) composition, 1936-1938 ....300.00
PANAMA   8" (20cm) hard plastic, 1985-1987 ....75.00
PANDORA   8" (20cm) hard plastic, made for Dolls 'n Bearland, 1991
(see Special Dolls) 85.00
PARLOUR MAID   8" (20cm) hard plastic, 1956 ....950.00 up
PATCHITY PAM & PEPPER   15" (38cm) cloth, 1965-1966 ....175.00
PATTERSON, MARTHA JOHNSON   3rd set, First Ladies Series, 1982-1984.........95.00
PATTY   18" (46cm) plastic, vinyl, 1965 ....225.00
PATTY PIGTAILS   14" (36cm) hard plastic, 1949 ....650.00
PAULETTE   10" (25cm), Portrette, 1989-1990 ....90.00
PEARL (JUNE)   10" (25cm), Birthstone Collection, 1992 ....64.00
PEASANT   7" (18cm) composition, 1936-1937 ....265.00
9" (23cm) composition, 1938-1939 ....285.00
PEGGY BRIDE   14-18" (36-46cm) hard plastic, 1950-1951 ....575.00 up
21" (53cm) hard plastic, 1950 ....750.00
PENNY   7" (18cm) composition, 1938-1940..285.00
34" (86cm) cloth, vinyl, 1951 ....450.00
42" (106cm), 1951 ....600.00
PERSIA   7" (18cm) composition, 1936-1938 ....300.00
PERU   8" (20cm), 1986-1987 ....90.00
8" (20cm), International Dolls, 1993 ....50.00
PERUVIAN BOY   8" (20cm) hard plastic, bend knee, 1965-1966 ....400.00
8" (20cm) hard plastic, bend knee walker...475.00
PETER PAN   8" (20cm) hard plastic, Quiz-Kins, 1953 ....1200.00
15" (38cm) hard plastic, 1953-1954 ....800.00
14" (36cm) plastic, vinyl, 1969..300.00
Complete set of four dolls (Peter, Michael, Wendy, Tinkerbelle), 1969 .....900.00 up
8" (20cm) hard plastic, Storyland Dolls, re-introduced 1991-1993 ....52.00
PHILIPPINES   8" (20cm) straight leg, 1986-1987 ....85.00
yellow gown, 1987 ....125.00
PIERCE, JANE   3rd set, First Ladies Series, 1982-1984 ....95.00
PIERROT CLOWN   8" (20cm) hard plastic, 1956 ....950.00 up
14" (36cm), Classic Dolls, 1991-1992 ....80.00
PILGRIM   7" (18cm) composition, 1935-1938..275.00
PINK CHAMPAGNE   18" (46cm) hard plastic, 1950 ....3000.00
PINKY   16" (41cm) cloth, 1940s 475.00
23" (58cm) composition, cloth baby, 1937-1939 ....250.00
13-19" (33-48cm) vinyl baby, 1954 ....65.00-95.00
12" (31cm) plastic, vinyl, Portrait Children Series, 1975-1987 ....65.00
PINOCCHIO   8" (20cm), Storyland Dolls, 1992-1993 ....55.00
PIP   all cloth, Dicken's character, early 1930s 800.00
7" (18cm) composition, 1935-1936 ....285.00
PITTY PAT   16" (41cm) cloth, 1950s 400.00
PITTY PAT CLOWN   1950s 450.00
PLAYMATES   29" (74cm) cloth, 1940s 450.00

POCAHONTAS 8" (20cm) hard plastic, bend knee, Americana and
Storyland Dolls, 1967-1970 .... $ 375.00
  8" (20cm) hard plastic, Americana Series, re-introduced 1991 .... 52.00
POLISH (POLAND) 7" (18cm) composition, 1935-1936 .... 250.00
  8" (20cm) hard plastic, bend knee walker, 1964-1965 .... 200.00
  8" (20cm) hard plastic, bend knee, 1965-1972 .... 135.00
  8" (20cm) hard plastic, straight leg, 1973-1975 .... 60.00
  8" (20cm) hard plastic, straight leg, 1976-1988 .... 45.00
  8" (20cm) hard plastic, re-introduced 1992-1993 .... 65.00
POLK, SARAH 2nd set, First Ladies Series, 1979-1981 .... 105.00
POLLERA (PAN AMERICAN) 7" (18cm) composition, 1936-1937 .... 285.00
POLLY 17" (43cm) plastic, vinyl, 1965 .... 325.00
  plastic, vinyl, Ballerina 300.00
  plastic, vinyl, Ballgown 400.00
  plastic, vinyl, Bride 325.00
  plastic, vinyl, Street dress 325.00
  plastic, vinyl, in Trunk, wardrobe, 1965 .... 800.00
POLLY FLINDERS 8" (20cm), Storyland Dolls, 1988-1989 .... 90.00
POLLY PIGTAILS 14" (36cm) hard plastic, 1949-1951 .... 475.00
  17" (43cm), 1949-1951 .... 600.00
  8" (20cm) hard plastic, MADC, 1990 (*see Special Dolls*) 175.00

Long a friend of collectors,
The Enchanted Doll House
in Manchester Center, Ver-
mont, had Alexander Doll
Company exclusives. This
early 1980s 8in (20cm) doll
was dressed in the En-
chanted Doll House pink
check logo costume. Later,
a 10in (20cm) doll was offered as well.

The 1987 Madame Alexander Doll Club Convention in San Antonio, Texas, had this adorable 8in (20cm) *Cowboy* as its first ever Alexander Doll Company tagged souvenir.

17-18" (43-46cm) hard plastic, 1948-1950	$ 875.00
21" (53cm) hard plastic, 1949-1951	975.00
12" (31cm) hard plastic, Romance Collection, 1990-1991	90.00
8" (20cm), Storyland Dolls, 1993	70.00
PRINCE PHILLIP 18" (46cm) hard plastic, 1953	750.00
21" (53cm), 1953	850.00
PRINCESS 14" (36cm) plastic, vinyl, 1990-1991	140.00
12" (31cm) plastic, vinyl, Romance Collection, 1990-1992	92.00
PRINCESS ALEXANDRIA 24" (61cm) cloth, composition, 1937	225.00 up
PRINCESS AND THE PEA 8" (20cm) hard plastic, made for Dolly Dears, 1993	
(*see Special Dolls*)	80.00
PRINCESS ANN 8" (20cm) hard plastic, 1957	800.00
PRINCESS BUDIR AL-BUDIR 8" (20cm), Storyland Dolls, 1993	70.00
PRINCESS DOLL 13-15" (33-38cm) composition, 1940-1942	525.00
24" (61cm) composition, 1940-1942	775.00
PRINCESS ELIZABETH 7" (18cm) composition, 1937-1939	300.00
8" (20cm) with Dionne head, 1937 (rare)	350.00
9-11" (23-28cm) composition, 1937-1941	350.00-400.00
13" (33cm) composition with closed mouth, 1937-1941	500.00

For 1988, the Alexander Doll Company made for the Madame Alexander Doll Club a standard line doll called *Flapper* in a 10in (25cm) size using the standard mold going back to 1957, but dressed in black.

14" (36cm) composition, 1937-1941	$ 500.00
15" (38cm) composition, open mouth, 1937-1941	525.00
18-19" (46-48cm) composition, open mouth, 1937-1941	625.00
24" (61cm) composition, open mouth, 1938-1939	750.00
28" (71cm) composition, open mouth, 1938-1939	950.00

PRINCESS FLAVIA 21" (53cm) composition, 1939,
1946-1947 .... 1800.00 up
PRINCESS MARGARET ROSE 15-18" (38-46cm) composition, 1937-1938 .... 775.00
    21" (53cm) composition, 1938 .... 965.00
    14-18" (36-46cm) hard plastic, 1949-1953 .... 775.00
    18" (46cm) hard plastic, pink taffeta gown and tiara, Beaux Art Series,
    1953 .... 1300.00
PRINCESS ROSETTA 21" (53cm) composition, 1939, 1946-1947 .... 1500.00
PRISCILLA 18" (46cm) cloth, mid 1930s 650.00
    7" (18cm) composition, 1935-1938 .... 285.00
    8" (20cm) hard plastic, bend knee, Americana and Storyland Dolls,
    1965-1970 .... 375.00
PRISSY 8" (20cm), Scarlett Series, 1990 .... 57.00
    8" (20cm), re-introduced 1992-1993 .... 50.00

Always the star, Madame Alexander herself was the subject of this collector 21in (53cm) Portrait doll from the late 1980s. It used a special mold and is still undervalued and a great buy. Expect the price of this doll to rise drastically in the future.

Prom Queen 8" (20cm), MADC, 1992 (*see Special Dolls*) ....$ 275.00
Puddin' 14-21" (36-53cm) cloth, vinyl, 1966-1975 ....85.00
    14-18" (36-46cm), 1987 ....75.00
    14-21" (36-53cm), 1990-1993 ....95.00-105.00
Pumpkin 22" (56cm) cloth, vinyl, 1967-1976.. 145.00
    22" (56cm) with rooted hair, 1976 .... 165.00
Pussy Cat 14-18" (36-46cm) cloth, vinyl, 1965-1992................................95.00
    Lively, 14" (36cm), 20" (51cm), 24" (61cm), head and limbs move,
        1966-1969 ....95.00
    14" (36cm) black, 1974-1979 ....95.00
    14" (36cm) black, re-introduced 1991-1992....................................85.00-105.00
    14" (36cm), in trunk, trousseau, 1966, 1968 ....350.00 up
    20" (51cm) white, black 100.00
    24" (61cm) 125.00
Pussy Cat 18" (46cm), made for FAO Schwarz, 1987 (*see Special Dolls*) 125.00

Gary Green of Atlanta, Georgia, sponsors a gathering of collectors each summer
for subscribers to his doll newsletter. Gary and wife Dian's daughter, *Tippi*, was
the first Alexander Doll Company doll manufactured for this show in 1988.

Q QUEEN 18" (46cm) hard plastic, white gown, velvet long cape trimmed with fur, Beaux Arts Series, 1953 ....$ 1200.00
18" (46cm) hard plastic, same gown, tiara as above but no cape, Glamour Girl Series, 1953 ....700.00
18" (46cm) hard plastic, white gown, short orlon cape, Me and My Shadow Series, 1954 ....950.00
8" (20cm) hard plastic, orlon cape attached to purple robe, Me & My Shadow Series, 1954 ....950.00 up
20" (51cm) hard plastic, vinyl arms, white brocade, Dream Come True Series, 1955 ....850.00
8" (20cm) velvet robe, 1955 ....700.00
21" (53cm), white gown, Fashion Parade Series, 1957 ....850.00
10" (25cm) hard plastic, gold gown, blue sash, 1957 ....350.00
10" (25cm), gold gown, panels on back of dress 350.00
10" (25cm), white gowns, blue sash, 1959-1963 ....450.00
10" (25cm), in trunk, wardrobe, 1959 ....900.00 up
18" (46cm) Elise, white gown, red sash, 1963 ....750.00
With vinyl head 775.00
21" (53cm), gold gown, 1958, 1961-1963 ....800.00
18" (46cm) vinyl head, gold brocade gown, same as 1965, rare, (21" [53cm], rooted hair, 1966) 950.00
21" (53cm) hard plastic, vinyl arms, gold brocade gown, 1965 ....750.00
Gold gown, 1968 ....700.00
10" (25cm) hard plastic, white gowns, red sash, 1972-1974 ....350.00
14" (36cm), Classic Dolls, 1990 ....90.00
QUEEN ALEXANDRINE 21" (53cm) composition, 1939-1941 ....1700.00
QUEEN CHARLOTTE 10" (25cm), MADC, 1991 (*see Special Dolls*) 300.00
QUEEN ELIZABETH I 10" (25cm), made for My Doll House, 1990 (*see Special Dolls*) 200.00
QUEEN ELIZABETH II 8" (20cm),40th anniversary, mid-year release, 1992 (*see Special Dolls*) 130.00
QUEEN ISABELLA 21" (53cm), one-of-a-kind, Disney World Auction, 1991 (*see Special Dolls*) 6750.00
QUEEN OF HEARTS 8" (20cm) straight leg, Storyland Dolls, 1987-1990.........90.00
10" (25cm), Disney®, #4 Annual Showcase of Dolls, 1992 (*see Special Dolls*) 475.00
QUINTUPLETS (SO CALLED FISHER QUINTS) hard plastic, 1964 ....600.00 set
QUIZ-KINS 8" (20cm) hard plastic, in romper, 1953 ....475.00
Bride, 1953-1954 ....650.00
Girl with wig, 1953-1954 ....550.00
Groom, 1953-1954 ....500.00
Peter Pan, caracul wig, 1953 ....750.00

R RACHEL 8" (20cm), a few tagged Rachael, made for Belk & Leggett, 1989 (*see Special Dolls*) 75.00
RANDOLPH, MARTHA 1st set, First Ladies Series, 1976-1978 ....120.00
RAPUNZEL 10" (25cm), Portrette, 1989-1992 ....115.00
RAPUNZEL & MOTHER GOTHEL 14" (36cm), 8" (20cm), Classic Dolls, 1993 ....250.00
REBECCA 14-17" (36-43cm), 21" (53cm) composition, 1940-1941 ....550.00, 950.00
14" (36cm) hard plastic, 1948-1949 ....900.00
14" (36cm) plastic, vinyl, two-tiered skirt in pink, Classic Dolls, 1968-1969 ....250.00

one-piece skirt, pink dotted or checked dress, 1970-1985 .... $ 75.00
blue dress with striped pinafore, 1986-1987 .... 60.00
RED BOY　8" (20cm) hard plastic, bend knee, 1972 .... 100.00
1973-1975, straight leg 60.00
1976-1988, straight leg 55.00
RED CROSS NURSE　7" (18cm) composition, 1937, 1941-1943 .... 285.00
9" (23cm) composition, 1939, 1942-1943 .... 300.00
14" (36cm) hard plastic, 1948 .... 875.00
RED RIDING HOOD　16" (41cm) cloth, felt, 1930s 650.00
7" (18cm) composition, 1936-1942 .... 285.00
9" (23cm) composition, 1939-1940 .... 300.00
8" (20cm) hard plastic, straight leg walker, 1955 .... 375.00
8" (20cm) hard plastic, bend knee walker, Storyland Dolls, 1962-1965 ..... 325.00
8" (20cm) hard plastic, bend knee, 1965-1972 .... 135.00
8" (20cm) hard plastic, straight leg, 1973-1975 .... 60.00
8" (20cm) hard plastic, straight leg, 1976-1986 .... 55.00
8" (20cm), 1987-1993 .... 55.00

Miss Leigh was the second Alexander Doll Company special doll for the Collector's United Gathering in 1989. This doll was modeled after Gary and Dian's daughter, Leigh.

RENOIR 21" (53cm) composition, 1945-1946 ....$ 1800.00
  14" (36cm) hard plastic, 1950 ....875.00
  21" (53cm) hard plastic, vinyl arms, 1961 .... 850.00
  18" (46cm) hard plastic, vinyl arms, vinyl head, 1963 ....600.00
  21" (53cm) hard plastic, vinyl arms, pink gown, 1965 ....700.00
  21" (53cm), blue gown with black trim, 1966 ....1800.00
  21" (53cm), navy blue gown, red hat, 1967 ....650.00
  10" (25cm) hard plastic, all navy with red hat, 1968 ....450.00
  21" (53cm), yellow gown, full lace overdress, 1969-1970 ....650.00
  10" (25cm), pale blue gown, short jacket, stripe or dotted skirt, 1969 ....500.00
  10" (25cm), all aqua satin, 1970 ....450.00
  21" (53cm), all yellow two-piece gown pleated under skirt, 1971 ....650.00
  21" (53cm), pink gown with black jacket and trim, 1972...........................650.00
  21" (53cm) hard plastic, vinyl arms, yellow gold gown, black
  ribbon, 1973 ....625.00
RENOIR CHILD   12" (31cm) plastic, vinyl, Portrait Children Series, 1967......165.00
  14" (36cm), 1968 ....200.00
RENOIR GIRL   14" (36cm) plastic, vinyl, white dress, red ribbon trim,
Portrait Children Series, 1967-1968 ....200.00

In 1990, the Green's daughter *Shea* was the star at the Collector's United Gathering as a Christmas elf. This doll, like all of the Collector's United Gathering special dolls, was 8in (20cm) tall.

Pink dress, white pinafore, 1969-1971 .... $ 90.00
Pink multi-tiered lace gown, 1972-1986 ....70.00
Pink pleated nylon dress, 1986 ....70.00
RENOIR GIRL WITH WATERING CAN   Classic Dolls and
Fine Arts Series, 1986-1987 ....75.00
With hoop, Classic Dolls and Fine Arts Series, 1986-1987 ....75.00
RHETT   12" (31cm) plastic, vinyl, Portrait Children Series, 1981-1985 ....85.00
8" (20cm) hard plastic, Jubilee II, 1989 ....95.00
8" (20cm) hard plastic, Scarlett Series, 1991-1993 ....57.00
RIDING HABIT   8" (20cm), Americana Series, 1990 ....90.00
RILEY'S LITTLE ANNIE   14" (36cm) plastic, vinyl, Literature Series, 1967 ....175.00
RINGBEARER   14" (36cm) hard plastic, 1951 ....500.00
RING MASTER   8" (20cm) hard plastic, CU Gathering, 1991 (*see Special Dolls*) 175.00
RIVERBOAT QUEEN - LENA   8" (20cm) hard plastic, MADC, 1990
(*see Special Dolls*) 375.00
ROBIN HOOD   8" (20cm), Storyland Dolls, 1988-1990 ....85.00
RODEO   8" (20cm) hard plastic, 1955 ....900.00
ROLLER SKATING   8" (20cm) hard plastic, 1953-1955 ....500.00
ROMANCE   21" (53cm) composition, 1945-1946 ....1500.00
ROMEO   18" (46cm) composition, 1949 ....1200.00
8" (20cm) hard plastic, 1955 ....950.00 up

Reissued almost identically from the late 1960s, this late 1980s *English Guard* was a surprise to collectors. The Alexander Doll Company today is most interested in preserving the fond memories associated with some of their earlier products.

12" (31cm) plastic, vinyl, Portrait Children Series, 1978-1987 .... $ 45.00
12" (31cm) re-introduced, Romance Series, 1991-1992 .... 92.00
ROOSEVELT, EDITH 5th set, First Ladies Series, 1988 .... 85.00
ROOSEVELT, ELEANOR 14" (36cm) plastic, vinyl, 6th set, First Ladies
Series, 1989-1990 .... 100.00
ROSAMUND BRIDESMAID 15" (38cm) hard plastic, 1951 .... 475.00
18" (46cm) hard plastic, 1951 .... 575.00
ROSE 9" (23cm) early vinyl toddler, pink organdy dress and bonnet, 1953 .. 100.00
ROSEBUD 16-19" (41-48cm) cloth, vinyl, 1952-1953 .... 135.00
13" (33cm), 1953 .... 160.00
23-25" (58-64cm), 1953 .... 185.00
ROSEBUD 14-20" (36-51cm), white, 1986 .... 60.00
14" (36cm), black 65.00
ROSE FAIRY 8" (20cm) hard plastic, 1956 .... 1200.00 up
ROSETTE 10" (25cm), Portrette Series, 1987-1989 .... 75.00
ROSEY POSEY 14" (36cm) cloth, vinyl, 1976 .... 65.00
21" (53cm) cloth, vinyl, 1976 .... 95.00
ROSS, BETSY 8" (20cm) hard plastic, bend knee, Americana Series,
1967-1972 .... 135.00
1976 Bicentennial gown with star print 125.00
Straight legs, Storyland Dolls, 1973-1975 .... 60.00
Straight legs, 1976-1987 .... 55.00
8" (20cm) re-introduced, Americana Series, 1991-1992 .... 55.00
ROSY 14" (36cm), 1988-1990 .... 75.00
ROUND UP DAY MOUSEKETEER 8" (20cm), made for Disney®, 1992
(*see Special Dolls*) 80.00
ROYAL WEDDING 21" (53cm) composition, 1939 .... 1500.00 up
ROZY 12" (31cm) plastic, vinyl, 1969 .... 450.00

This incredible set of twins called *Diana* and *David*, are 8in (20cm) size dolls and were made in 1989 as an F.A.O. Schwarz exclusive. The wagon is as adorable as the dolls and came with the set.

RUBY (JULY) 10" (25cm) hard plastic, Birthstone Collection, 1992 ....$ 64.00
RUFFLES CLOWN 21" (53cm), 1954 ....400.00
RUMANIA 8" (20cm) hard plastic, bend knee, 1968-1972 ....125.00
    8" (20cm) straight leg, 1973-1975 ....60.00
    8" (20cm) straight leg, 1976-1987 ....55.00
    8" (20cm), white face, 1986 ....55.00
RUMBERA, RUMBERO 7" (18cm) composition, 1938-1943 ....235.00 each
    9" (23cm) composition, 1939-1941 ....300.00 each
RUMPELSTILTSKIN & MILLER'S DAUGHTER 8" (20cm) and 14" (36cm),
    limited to 3000 sets, 1992 ....250.00
RUSSIA 8" (20cm) hard plastic, bend knee, 1968-1972 ....125.00
    8" (20cm) straight leg, 1973-1975 ....60.00
    8" (20cm) straight leg, 1976-1988 ....55.00
    8" (20cm), white face, 1985-1987 ....55.00
    8" (20cm), re-introduced 1991-1992 ....52.00
RUSSIAN 7" (18cm) composition, 1935-1938 ....265.00
RUSTY 20" (51cm) cloth, vinyl, 1967-1968 ....350.00

A beautiful 8in (20cm) *Scarlett* was selected as the 1990 Madame Alexander Doll
Club Symposium doll. Her parasol and wrist tag made her a special doll.

S SAILOR   14" (36cm) composition, 1942-1945 ....$ 750.00
17" (43cm) composition, 1943-1944 ....900.00
8" (20cm) boy, UFDC, 1990 (*see Special Dolls*) 700.00
8" (20cm) hard plastic, boy, made for FAO Schwarz, 1991 (*see Special Dolls*) 95.00
12" (31cm) hard plastic, *Classic Lissy*, see *Columbian Sailor*, UFDC,
 1993 (*see Special Dolls*) 350.00
SAILORETTE   10" (25cm) hard plastic, Portrette Series, 1988 ....75.00
SAKS OWN CHRISTMAS CAROL   8in (20cm) hard plastic, made for Saks
 Fifth Ave, 1993 (*see Special Dolls*) 70.00
SALLY BRIDE   14" (36cm) composition, 1938-1939 ....425.00
18-21" (46-53cm) composition, 1938-1939 ....485.00-650.00
SALOME   14" (36cm), Opera Series, 1984-1986 ....90.00
SAMANTHA   14" (36cm), made for FAO Schwarz, 1989 (*see Special Dolls*) ..110.00
14" (36cm), gold ruffled gown, Classic Dolls, 1991-1992 ....170.00
SANDY MCHARE   cloth, felt, 1930s 650.00
SAPPHIRE (SEPTEMBER)   10" (25cm) hard plastic, Birthstone Collection, 1992 ....64.00
SARDINIA   8" (20cm) hard plastic, 1989-1991 ....55.00
SARGENT   14" (36cm) plastic, vinyl, dressed in lavender, Fine Arts Series,
 1984-1985 ....75.00
SARGENT'S GIRL   14" (36cm) plastic, vinyl, dressed in pink, Fine Arts Series, 1986 .75.00
SCARECROW   8" (20cm) hard plastic, Storyland Dolls, 1993 ....55.00
SCARLETT O'HARA   (pre-movie, 1937-1938)
7" (18cm) composition, 1937-1942 ....425.00 up
11" (28cm) composition, 1937-1942 ....550.00
9" (23cm) composition, 1938-1941 ....475.00
18" (46cm) composition, 1939-1946 ....1000.00
14-15" (36-38cm) composition, 1941-1943 ....800.00
21" (53cm) composition, 1945, 1947 ....1400.00
8" (20cm) hard plastic, white gown with red rosebuds, white lace hat,
 1953-1954 ....1000.00
8" (20cm) hard plastic, two layer gown, white, yellow, green
 trim, 1955 ....950.00
8" (20cm) hard plastic, straight leg walker, pink or blue floral gown,
 1956..950.00
8" (20cm) hard plastic, bend knee walker, white, lace and ribbon trim,
 1957..950.00
20" (51cm), jointed arm, Cissy, Scarlett with deep green velvet gown,
 matching jacket and bonnet trimmed in light green net, 1958 (rare) .... 1400.00 up
21" (53cm) Cissy, Scarlett with straight arms, gown of white organdy
 trimmed with lace beading apple green inserted ribbons on tiers
 of skirt, white horsehair braid picture hat, 1961 (rare) .... 1400.00 up
21" (53cm) Cissy, Scarlett straight arms, blue taffeta gown with
 black braid trim with matching coat and bonnet, 1961 ....1300.00 up
12" (31cm) hard plastic, green taffeta gown and bonnet, 1963 (rare) ....1400.00 up
18" (46cm) hard plastic, vinyl arms, pale blue organdy with rosebuds
 and straw hat, 1963 only ....1000.00 up
8" (20cm) hard plastic, bend knee, in white gown, 1965............................750.00
21" (53cm) hard plastic, vinyl arms, green taffeta gown, 1965 ....1200.00 up
8" (20cm) hard plastic, bend knee, flowered gown, Americana and
 Storyland Dolls, 1966-1972 ....350.00 up
21" (53cm) plastic, vinyl, all white gown, red sash and roses variations,
 1966 (referred to as Coco) 2700.00
21" (53cm) plastic, vinyl, green taffeta gown with black trim, 1967 ....650.00
10" (25cm) hard plastic, lace in bonnet, green taffeta gown with black
 braid trim, 1968 ....475.00

14" (36cm) plastic, vinyl, floral gown, 1968 .... $ 450.00
14" (36cm) plastic, vinyl, white gown with rows of lace, 1968-1986 .... 90.00
21" (53cm) plastic, vinyl, floral print gown with wide white hem, 1968 .. 1000.00
10" (25cm) hard plastic, green taffeta gown with white and gold
   braid trim, 1969 .... 450.00
21" (53cm) plastic, vinyl, green taffeta white braid trim, 1969 .... 500.00
10" (25cm) hard plastic, green taffeta gown with gold braid trim, 1970-1973 ...... 450.00
21" (53cm) plastic, vinyl, green taffeta, white trim on jacket, 1970 .... 725.00
8" (20cm) hard plastic, in white gown, 1973-1992 .... 65.00
21" (53cm) plastic, vinyl, all green taffeta, white lace at cuffs, 1975-1977 .... 450.00
21" (53cm) plastic, vinyl, silk floral gown, green parasol, white lace, 1978 ... 400.00
21" (53cm) plastic, vinyl, green velvet, 1979-1985 .... 325.00
12" (31cm) plastic, vinyl, green gown with braid trim, 1981-1985 .... 85.00
8" (20cm) hard plastic, white gown with red sash, MADC, 1986
   (*see Special Dolls*) 250.00
14" (36cm) plastic, vinyl, Jubilee #1, all green velvet, 1986 .... 165.00
21" (53cm) plastic, vinyl, floral gown, green parasol, 1986 .... 350.00
8" (20cm) hard plastic, white face, blue dot gown, 1987 .... 225.00
21" (53cm) plastic, vinyl, layered all over white gown, 1987-1988 .... 325.00
14" (36cm) plastic, vinyl, blue floral print, 1987-1989 .... 145.00
8" (20cm) hard plastic, straight leg, flowered gown, 1988-1989 .... 60.00
8" (20cm) hard plastic, Jubilee #2, all green velvet gown, 1989 .... 145.00
10" (25cm) hard plastic, Jubilee #2, burgundy and white gown, 1989 .... 100.00

1989 found this special 10in (25cm) *Cinderella* still being a classic. She was offered to attendees at the 1989 Walt Disney® World Doll and Teddy Bear Convention.

Scarlett continued from page 103.

14" (36cm) plastic, vinyl, Jubilee #2, green floral print gown, 1989 ....$100.00
21" (53cm) plastic, vinyl, red gown, 1989 (birthday party dress) 300.00
8" (20cm) hard plastic, MADC Symposium, 1990 (*see Special Dolls*) 200.00
8" (20cm) hard plastic, straight leg, tiny floral print, 1990 ....60.00
14" (36cm) plastic, vinyl, tiny floral print gown, Scarlett Series, 1990 ......135.00
10" (25cm) hard plastic, floral print gown, Scarlett Series, 1990-1991 ....85.00
21" (53cm) plastic, vinyl, Bride, Scarlett Series, 1990-1993 ....355.00
8" (20cm) hard plastic, four-tier white gown, curly hair, 1991 only 65.00
21" (53cm) porcelain, green velvet, gold trim, 1991 ....585.00
14" (36cm) plastic, vinyl, white ruffles, green ribbon, Scarlett Series,
   1991-1992 ....147.00
21" (53cm) plastic, vinyl, green on white, three ruffles around skirt,
   1991-1992 ....295.00
8" (20cm) hard plastic, rose floral print, oversized bonnet, 1992 ....65.00
10" (25cm) hard plastic, Scarlett at the Ball, all in black, 1992 ....90.00
8" (20cm) hard plastic, green and white stripe gown, 1993 ....60.00
8" (20cm) hard plastic, in trunk, "Honeymoon in New Orleans," 1993 ......175.00
8" (20cm) hard plastic, 70th Anniversary, mid year release, 1993 ....70.00
10" (25cm) hard plastic, green velvet with gold trim, 1993 ....100.00

Diamond Lil was the incredible 10in (25cm) souvenir doll at the Madame Alexander Doll Club Convention in Kansas City, 1993.

SCHOOL GIRL   7" (18cm) composition, 1936-1943 ....$ 285.00
SCOTCH   7" (18cm) composition, 1936-1939...265.00
    9" (23cm) composition, 1939-1940 ....285.00
    10" (25cm) hard plastic, 1962-1963 ....750.00 up
SCOTS LASS   8" (20cm) hard plastic, bend knee walker, 1963 ....250.00
SCOTTISH (SCOTLAND)   8" (20cm) hard plastic, bend knee walker,
    1964-1965 ....200.00
    8" (20cm) hard plastic, bend knee, 1965-1972 ....125.00
    8" (20cm) straight leg, 1973-1975 ....60.00
    8" (20cm) straight leg, 1976-1993 ....52.00
SCOUTING   8" (20cm) hard plastic, Americana Series, 1991-1992 ....55.00
SEPTEMBER   14" (36cm) plastic, vinyl, Classic Dolls, 1989 ....75.00
SEVEN DWARFS   9" (23cm) composition, 1937 ....450.00 each
SHAHARAZAD   10" (25cm) hard plastic, Portrette Series, 1992-1993 ....84.00
SHEA   8" (20cm) hard plastic, elf, CU Gathering, 1990 (see Special Dolls) ..200.00
SICILY   8" (20cm) hard plastic, 1989-1990 ....75.00
SIMONE   21" (53cm) hard plastic, vinyl arms, in trunk, 1968
    (same doll as Jacqueline) 1800.00
SIR LAPIN HARE   cloth, felt, 1930s 650.00
SISTER BRENDA   8" (20cm) hard plastic, made for FAO Schwarz,
    (see Special Dolls) 230.00

Cecila's Dolls had *David, the Little Rabbi* as its special doll in 1991. By using the 8in (20cm) doll as its theme, *David* will be a valuable collectible in the future.

Sitting Pretty   18" (46cm) cloth body, 1965 (rare) ....$ 350.00
Skater   15-18" (38-46cm) hard plastic, vinyl, 1955-1956 ....600.00
Sleeping Beauty   7-9" (18-23cm) composition, 1941-1944 ....300.00
   15-16" (38-41cm) composition, 1938-1940 ....400.00
   18-21" (46-53cm) composition, 1941-1944 ....550.00
   16 ½" (42cm) hard plastic, 1959 ....550.00
   21" (53cm) hard plastic, 1959 ....875.00
   10" (25cm) hard plastic, 1959-1960 ....450.00
   14" (36cm) plastic, vinyl, gold gown, Classic Dolls, 1971-1985 ....75.00
   14" (36cm) plastic, vinyl, blue gown, Classic Dolls, 1986-1990 ....90.00
   10" (25cm) hard plastic, Portrette Series, 1991-1992 ....95.00
   21" (53cm) plastic vinyl, Disneyworld® Auction, 1989 (*see Special Dolls*) .2950.00
Slumbermate   12" (31cm) cloth/composition, 1940s 175.00
   13" (33cm) vinyl, cloth, 1951 ....125.00
   21" (53cm) composition, cloth, 1940s 250.00
Smarty   12" (31cm) plastic, vinyl, 1962-1963 ....275.00
   Smarty & Baby, 1963 (rare) 300.00
   With boy "Artie" in case with wardrobe, 1963 (very rare)......................1000.00 up
Smee   8" (20cm), Storyland Dolls, 1993 ....55.00
Smiley   20" (51cm) cloth, vinyl, 1971 ....265.00
Smokey Tail   cloth, felt, 1930s 650.00
Snow Flake   10" (25cm) hard plastic, Portrette Series, 1993 ....85.00
Snow Queen   10" (25cm) hard plastic, Portrette Series, 1991-1992................84.00
Snow White   12" (31cm) composition, 1939-1940 ....400.00
   13" (33cm) composition, painted eyes, 1937-1939 ....400.00
   13" (33cm) composition, sleep eyes, 1939-1940 ....385.00
   16" (41cm) composition, 1939-1942 ....475.00

1992's Dolly Dear's Doll Artist Show special doll was *Susanna*. Her tiny 8in (20cm) size belies the fact that she is an excellent "clogger," as evidenced by the tiny little "cloggs" on her shoes. Her special centerpiece and hand-dressed companion were delightful table favors. Centerpiece by Floyd and Gracie James. Companion doll dressed by Liz Toms and Fran Clinkscals.

18" (46cm) composition, 1939-1940 .... $ 600.00
15-18-23" (46-58cm) hard plastic, 1952 .... 650.00-800.00-950.00
14" (36cm) plastic, vinyl, white gown, Classic Dolls, 1968-1985 .... 150.00
   ecru and gold gown, red cape, 1986-1992 .... 120.00
14" (36cm) plastic, vinyl, Disney® Colors, 1967-1977 .... 375.00
8" (20cm) hard plastic, Disney® Colors, 1972-1976 (*see Special Dolls*) 475.00
12" (31cm) plastic, vinyl, made for Disney®, 1990 (*see Special Dolls*) 250.00
8" (20cm), Storyland Dolls, 1990-1992 .... 55.00
SNOW WHITE   Disneyland®, 1993 (*see Special Dolls*) .... N/A
SO BIG   22" (56cm) cloth, vinyl, painted eyes, 1968-1975 .... 250.00
SO LITE BABY OR TODDLER   20" (51cm) cloth, 1930s .... 450.00 up
SOLDIER   14" (36cm) composition, 1943-1944 .... 750.00
   17" (43cm) composition, 1942-1945 .... 850.00
SOUND OF MUSIC   All in same outfit: red skirt, white attached
   blouse black vest that ties in front with gold thread,
   ca. 1965 (very rare) .... 350.00-500.00 up each

One of the most revolutionary dolls ever made by the Alexander Doll Company, is this African-American *Welcome Home* female 8in (20cm) doll. One of a group of six dolls, they were the mid-year release of the Alexander Doll Company in 1991.

107

SOUND OF MUSIC, DRESSED IN SAILOR SUITS & TAGGED, CA. 1965

10" (25cm) Friedrich ....$ 350.00
10" (25cm) Gretl 350.00
10" (25cm) Marta 350.00
14" (36cm) Louisa 475.00
14" (36cm) Brigitta 375.00
14" (36cm) Liesl 375.00
17" (43cm) Maria 475.00
Set of 7 dolls ....N/A

SOUND OF MUSIC, LARGE SET, 1965-1970

10" (25cm) Friedrich 175.00
10" (25cm) Marta, 10" (25cm) Gretl .... 175.00 each
14" (36cm) Brigitta, 14" (36cm) Liesl .... 175.00 each
14" (36cm) Louisa 300.00
17" (43cm) Maria 375.00
Full set of 7 dolls.. 1700.00

SOUND OF MUSIC, SMALL SET, 1971-1973

8" (20cm) Marta, 8" (20cm) Friedrich, 8" (20cm) Gretl .... 150.00 each
10" (25cm) Brigitta 225.00

Who could resist this adorable *Charlene* baby doll from 1992. While part of the regular Alexander Doll Company line, the head was sculpted by artist Hildegard Gunzel.

10" (25cm) Liesl .... $ 200.00
10" (25cm) Louisa.. 265.00
12" (31cm) Maria 300.00
Set of 7 dolls .... 1400.00 up

SOUND OF MUSIC, REINTRODUCED 1992-1993
8" (20cm) Brigitta 55.00
8" (20cm) Gretl and Kurt (boy in sailor suit)...................................... 62.00 each
10" (25cm) Maria 85.00
12" (31cm) Maria Bride 132.00

SOUND OF MUSIC 1993 (continuation of set)
8" (20cm) Friedrich... 55.00
8" (20cm) Marta.. 55.00
10" (25cm) Liesl 75.00
10" (25cm) Maria at the Abby 70.00

SOUTH AMERICAN   7" (18cm) composition, 1938-1943 .... 285.00
9" (23cm) composition, 1939-1941 .... 300.00

SOUTHERN BELLE OR GIRL   8" (20cm) hard plastic, 1953-1954 .... 950.00 up
8" (20cm) hard plastic, 1955 .... 750.00
8" (20cm) hard plastic, 1956 .... 900.00
8" (20cm) hard plastic, 1963 .... 450.00
12" (31cm) hard plastic, 1963 .... 1200.00

For 1992-93, the Alexander Doll Company is capturing everyone's hearts with another addition of Rogers and Hammerstein's *Sound of Music* dolls. *Maria* is beautifully executed in the 10in (25cm) size.

21" (53cm) hard plastic, vinyl arms, blue gown with wide pleated
hem, 1965 .... $ 900.00
White gown with green ribbon trim, 1967 .... 650.00
10" (25cm) hard plastic, white gown with green ribbon thru three
10" (25cm), rows of lace, 1968 .... 425.00
10" (25cm), white gown with rows of lace, pink sash, 1969 .... 425.00
10" (25cm) hard plastic, white gown with red ribbon sash, 1970 .... 425.00
10" (25cm) hard plastic, white gown with green ribbon sash, 1971-1973 .. 425.00
10" (25cm), made for My Doll House, 1989 (*see Special Dolls*) 200.00
SOUTHERN GIRL   11-14" (28-36cm) composition, 1940-1943 .... 475.00
17-21" (43-53cm) composition, 1940-1943 .... 650.00-750.00
SPANISH   7-8" (18-20cm) composition, 1935-1939 .... 265.00
9" (23cm) composition, 1936-1940 .... 285.00
SPANISH BOY   8" (20cm) hard plastic, bend knee and bend knee walker,
1964-1968 .... 350.00
SPANISH GIRL   8" (20cm) hard plastic, bend knee walker, three-tiered
skirt, 1962-1965 .... 150.00
8" (20cm) hard plastic, bend knee, three-tiered skirt, 1965-1972 .... 135.00
8" (20cm) straight leg, three-tiered skirt, 1973-1975 .... 85.00
8" (20cm) straight leg, three-tiered skirt, 1976-1982 .... 65.00
8" (20cm) straight leg, two-tiered skirt, 1983-1985 .... 55.00

The words "Walt Disney" combined with the talents of the Alexander Doll Company has made collectors very happy with these special dolls available at Disney World® and Disneyland®. From left, all 8in (20cm), *Round Up Day Mouseketeer*, 1992, *Mouseketeer*, 1991, and *Bobbie Sox*, 1990!

8" (20cm) straight leg, white with red polka dots, 1986 - 1989 .... $ 60.00
8" (20cm) straight leg, all red tiered skirt, 1990-1992 .... 55.00
Spanish Matador 8" (20cm), 1992-1993 .... 55.00
Special Girl 23-24" (58-61cm) cloth, composition, 1942-1946 .... 450.00
Spring 14" (36cm) plastic, vinyl, Classic Dolls, 1993 .... 150.00
Spring Break 8" (20cm) hard plastic, Metroplex Doll Club, 1992
(*see Special Dolls*) 350.00
Springtime 8" (20cm), MADC, 1991 (*see Special Dolls*) 200.00
Stilts 8" (20cm) hard plastic, clown on stilts, 1992-1993 .... 60.00
Story Princess 8" (20cm) hard plastic, 1956 .... 1200.00
15", 18" (38cm, 46cm) hard plastic, 1956 .... 750.00 up
15-18" (38-46cm) plastic, vinyl, 1954 .... 675.00 up
15" (38cm) plastic, vinyl, 1955 .... 650.00 up
Stuffy (*see Little Men*)
Suellen 14-17" (36-43cm) composition, 1937-1938 .... 950.00
12" (31cm), yellow multi-tiered skirt, Scarlett Series, 1990 .... 75.00
Suellen 12" (31cm), made for Jean's Dolls, 1992 (*see Special Dolls*) 150.00
Sugar Darlin' 14-18" (36-46cm) cloth, vinyl, 1964 .... 100.00
14" (36cm), 18" (46cm), 24" (61cm), Lively, knob makes head
and limbs move, 1964 .... 125.00-165.00
24" (61cm), 1964 .... 150.00
Sugar Plum Fairy 10" (25cm), Portrette Series, 1992-1993 .... 92.00
Sugar Tears 12" (31cm) vinyl baby, 1964 .... 95.00

A VERY special set is this 10in (25cm) *Alice* and her factory made and labeled, *White Rabbit*. They were offered at the 1991 Walt Disney World® Doll and Teddy Bear Convention.

SULKY SUE   8" (20cm), 1988-1990 ....$ 90.00
SUMMER   14" (36cm), Classic Dolls, 1993 .... 135.00
SUNBONNET SUE   9" (23cm) composition, 1937-1940 .... 300.00
SUNFLOWER CLOWN   40" (101cm) all cloth, flower eyes, 1951 .... 800.00
SUSANNA   8" (20cm), made for Dolly Dears, 1992
   (*see Special Dolls*) 325.00
SUSIE Q   Cloth, 1940-1942 .... 650.00
SUZY   12" (31cm) plastic, vinyl, 1970 .... 350.00
SWEDEN (SWISS)   8" (20cm) hard plastic, bend knee walker, 1961-1965 .... 175.00
   8" (20cm), bend knee walker with smile face, 1963 .... 200.00
   8" (20cm) hard plastic, bend knee, 1965-1972 .... 125.00
   8" (20cm) straight leg, 1973-1975 .... 60.00
   8" (20cm) straight leg, 1976-1989 .... 55.00
   8" (20cm), white face, 1986 .... 55.00
   8" (20cm), reintroduced 1991 .... 55.00
SWEDISH   7" (18cm) composition, 1936-1940 .... 265.00
   9" (23cm) composition, 1937-1941 .... 285.00
   8" (20cm) hard plastic, bend knee, 1965-1969, 1972-1973 .... 125.00
SWEET BABY   18½-20" (47-51cm) cloth, latex, 1948 .... 40.00-50.00
SWEET BABY   14" (36cm), 1983-1984 .... 55.00
   14" (36cm), 1987-1993 .... 75.00
   14" (36cm) in carrycase, 1990-1992 .... 95.00-125.00
SWEET SIXTEEN   14" (36cm), Classic Dolls, 1991-1992 .... 120.00

Made in a very small edition of 250 pieces, this 8in (20cm) *Monique* is the first doll made for the premier 1993 Disneyland® Doll and Bear Classic. Because she is the first doll, and very limited, she will be quite valuable to future collectors.

Sweet Tears   9" (23cm) vinyl, 1965-1974 .... $ 50.00
   14" (36cm) in window box, 1965-1974 .... 145.00 up
   9" (23cm) vinyl, with layette in box, discontinued 1973 .... 150.00
   14" (36cm), 1965-1982 .... 55.00
   16" (41cm), 1965-1971 .... 85.00
   14" (36cm) in trunk, trousseau, 1967-1974 .... 200.00 up
   14" (36cm) with layette, 1979 .... 135.00
Sweet Violet   18" (46cm) hard plastic, jointed, 1954 only .... 700.00 up
Sweetie Baby   22" (56cm) all plastic, 1962 .... 145.00
Sweetie Walker   23" (58cm) all plastic, 1962 .... 245.00
Swiss   7" (18cm) composition, 1936 .... 265.00
   9" (23cm) composition, 1935-1938 .... 285.00
   10" (25cm) hard plastic, 1962-1963 .... 900.00
   8" (20cm) hard plastic, bend knee walker, (smile face), 1963 .... 200.00
   8" (20cm) hard plastic, bend knee, 1968-1972 .... 125.00
Switzerland   8" (20cm) hard plastic, bend knee walker, 1961-1965 .... 200.00
   8" (20cm) hard plastic, bend knee, 1965-1972 .... 135.00
   8" (20cm) hard plastic, straight leg, 1973-1975 .... 60.00
   8" (20cm) hard plastic, straight leg, 1976-1989 .... 55.00
   8" (20cm), white face, 1986 .... 55.00

A real collector's treasure is this 8in (20cm) 1989 *Wendy*, the first special Club Doll for The Madame Alexander Doll Club.

113

SYLVESTER THE JESTER   14" (36cm) plastic, vinyl, 1992-1993 ....$ 105.00

T TAFT, HELEN   5th set, First Ladies Series, 1988 ....85.00
TEENY TWINKLE   cloth, flirty eyes, 1946 ....500.00
TEXAS   8" (20cm), Americana Series, 1991 ....60.00
TEXAS SHRINER   8" (20cm) hard plastic, Shriners National Convention,
1993 (*see Special Dolls*) 525.00
THAILAND   8" (20cm) hard plastic, bend knee, 1966-1972 ....150.00
8" (20cm) straight leg, 1973-1975 ....60.00
8" (20cm) straight leg, 1976-1989 ....55.00
THOMAS, MARLO   17" (43cm) plastic, vinyl, 1967 (two versions) 600.00
THOROUGHLY MODERN WENDY   8" (20cm), made for Disney, 1992
(*see Special Dolls*) 70.00
THREE LITTLE PIGS   12" (31cm) composition, 1938-1939 .... 650.00 each
THUMBELINA & HER LADY   8" (20cm) hard plastic and 21" (53cm)
porcelain, limited edition of 2500 sets, 1992 ....550.00
TIBET   8" (20cm), International Dolls, 1993 ....50.00
TIGER LILY   8" (20cm), 1992-1993 ....55.00
TIMMY TODDLER   23" (58cm) plastic, vinyl, 1960-1961 ....150.00
30" (76cm), 1960 ....200.00
TIN WOODSMAN   8" (20cm), Storyland Dolls, 1993 ....55.00

1993 *Homecoming* 8in
(20cm) doll, a surprising
delight, was made for The
Madame Alexander Doll
Club Premiers. Stand made
by Ann Rast.

TINKERBELLE 11" (28cm) hard plastic, 1969 .... $ 450.00
   8" (20cm) hard plastic, Disney® Exclusive, 1973 (*see Special Dolls*) .... 950.00 up
   8" (20cm) hard plastic, magic wand, Storyland Dolls, 1991-1993 .... 65.00
TINY BETTY 7" (18cm) composition, 1935-1942 .... 285.00
TINY TIM Cloth, early 1930s 650.00
   7" (18cm) composition, 1934-1937 .... 350.00
   14" (36cm) composition, 1938-1940 .... 575.00
TIPPI 8" (20cm) hard plastic, CU Gathering, 1988 (*see Special Dolls*) 350.00
TIPPY TOE 16" (41cm) cloth, 1940s 600.00
TOM SAWYER 8" (20cm) hard plastic, Storyland Dolls, 1989-1990 .... 60.00
TOMMY 12" (31cm) hard plastic, made for FAO Schwarz
100th Anniversary, 1962 .... 1200.00
TOMMY BANGS (*see Little Men*)
TOMMY SNOOKS 8" (20cm) hard plastic, Storyland Dolls, 1988-1991 .... 55.00
TOMMY TITTLEMOUSE 8" (20cm) hard plastic, Storyland Dolls, 1988-1991 ... 55.00
TONY SARG MARIONETTES 12"-14" (31-36cm) composition, 1934-1940 ...... 145.00 up
TOPSY-TURVY 7"-9" (18cm-23cm) composition with Tiny Betty
heads, 1935 .... 165.00
   7" (18cm) with Dionne Quint head, 1936 .... 300.00
TOULOUSE-LAUTREC 21" (53cm) plastic, vinyl, black and pink, 1986-1987 .. 195.00

Looking very ready to sail the high seas, this 8in (20cm) *Sailor Boy* was the special doll made for the Alexander Luncheon at the 1990 United Federation of Doll Club, Inc. convention.

TOY SOLDIER 8" (20cm) hard plastic, Storyland Dolls, 1993 ....$ 55.00
TRAPEZE ARTIST 10" (25cm) hard plastic, Portrette Series, 1990-1991 ....95.00
TREE TOPPER 8" (20cm) hard plastic, dolls in cones without legs
  8" (20cm), red, 1990 ....65.00
  Merry Angel, made for Spiegel, 1991 (*see Special Dolls*)............................145.00
  Joy Noel, made for Spiegel, 1992 (*see Special Dolls*) 145.00
  8" (20cm), red, gold, 1992-1993 ....80.00
  Angel Lace, 1992-1993 ....65.00
  Red Velvet, 1993 ....85.00
  10" (25cm), Pink Victorian, 1993 ....75.00
TREENA BALLERINA 15" (38cm) hard plastic, 1952............................750.00
  18-21" (46-53cm), 1952..900.00
TRICK AND TREAT 8" (20cm) hard plastic, made for A Child at Heart, 1993
  (*see Special Dolls*) 145.00

Miss Unity was a fantastic collector surprise in a lady-like 10in (25cm) size! This
very special doll was the Alexander Luncheon souvenir at the 1991 U.F.D.C.,
Inc., convention. The wooden "Miss Unity" was a table favor. "Miss Unity" is
the registered logo of U.F.D.C., Inc.

Truman, Bess   14" (36cm) plastic, vinyl, 6th set, First Ladies Series, 1989-1990 ....$ 100.00
Tunisia   8" (20cm) hard plastic, 1989 ....75.00
Turkey   8" (20cm) hard plastic, bend knee, 1968-1972 ....125.00
  8" (20cm) straight leg, 1973-1975 ....60.00
  8" (20cm) straight leg, 1976-1986 ....55.00
Tweedledum & Tweedledee   14" (36cm) cloth, 1930-1931 ....700.00 each
20's Traveler   10" (25cm) hard plastic, Portrette Series, 1992 only 74.00
Tyler, Julia   2nd set, First Ladies Series, 1979-1981 ....105.00
Tyrolean Boy & Girl*   8" (20cm) hard plastic, bend knee walker, 1962-1965 ....175.00 each
  8" (20cm) hard plastic, bend knee, 1965-1972 ....135.00 each
  8" (20cm) straight leg, 1973 ....60.00 each
*Became Austria in 1974.

U.S.A.   8" (20cm) hard plastic, International Dolls, 1993 ....50.00
Union Officer   12" (31cm) hard plastic, vinyl, Scarlett Series, 1990-1991 ....80.00
Union Soldier   8" (20cm) hard plastic, Scarlett Series, 1991 ....85.00

Perfect for a San Francisco based convention, this 8in (20cm) *Little Emperor* was the Alexander Luncheon souvenir at the 1992 U.F.D.C., Inc. convention.

UNITED STATES   8" (20cm) hard plastic., 1974-1975 ....$ 50.00
    1976-1987 ....55.00
    1988-1992 ....50.00

V   **VAN BUREN, ANGELICA**   2nd set, First Ladies Series, 1979-1981 .... 105.00
     VERMONT MAIDEN   8" (20cm) hard plastic, made for Enchanted
        Doll House,1990 (*see Special Dolls*) 185.00
VICTORIA   21" (53cm) composition, 1939, 1941 .... 1800.00 up
    21" (53cm) composition, 1945-1946 .... 1800.00 up
    14" (36cm) hard plastic, 1950-1951 .... 950.00
    8" (20cm) hard plastic, matches 18" (46cm) doll, 1954 .... 950.00
    18" (46cm) hard plastic, blue gown, Me and My Shadow Series, 1954 .... 1200.00
VICTORIA (BABY)   18" (46cm) cloth, vinyl, baby, 1966 .... 55.00
    20" (51cm) cloth, vinyl, baby, 1967-1989 .... 75.00
    14" (36cm) cloth, vinyl, baby, 1975-1988, 1990-1993 .... 95.00
    20" (51cm) cloth, vinyl, baby, in dress, jacket, bonnet, 1986....................... 95.00
    14" (36cm) cloth, vinyl, baby, made for Lord & Taylor, 1989
        (*see Special Dolls*) 95.00
    18" (46cm) cloth, vinyl, baby, re-introduced, 1991-1993 .... 85.00

The 1893 World's Columbian Exposition was the theme of the U.F.D.C., Inc. convention. For the Alexander Luncheon, the Alexander Doll Company made an adorable 12in (31cm) hard plastic doll appropriately named *Columbian Sailor*.

VICTORIAN "so-called" 18" (46cm) hard plastic, pink taffeta and black
 velvet gown, Glamour Girl Series, 1953 ....$ 1200.00
VICTORIAN BRIDE 10" (25cm) hard plastic, Portrette Series, 1992 .... 105.00
VICTORIAN SKATER 10" (25cm) hard plastic, Portrette Series, 1993 .... 100.00
VIETNAM 8" (20cm) hard plastic, 1968-1969 ....250.00
 1968-1969 ....275.00
 8" (20cm), re-introduced in 1990-1991 ....55.00
VIOLETTA 10" (25cm) hard plastic, 1987-1988 ....60.00

W W.A.A.C. (ARMY) 14" (36cm) composition, 1943-1944 ....750.00
 W.A.A.F. (AIR FORCE) 14" (36cm) composition, 1943-1944 ....750.00
 W.A.V.E. (NAVY) 14" (36cm) composition, 1943-1944 ....750.00
WALTZING 8" (20cm) hard plastic, 1955 ....600.00
WASHINGTON, MARTHA 1st set, First Ladies Series, 1976-1978 ....275.00
WELCOME HOME (DESERT STORM) 8" (20cm) hard plastic, boy or girl
 soldier, black or white, blonde or brunette, mid-year release 1991 ....55.00 up each
WENDY (see Alexander-Kins)
 15" (38cm) hard plastic, 1955-1956 (Bride) 450.00
 18" (46cm) hard plastic, 1955-1956 (Bride) 650.00
 25" (64cm) hard plastic, 1955 (Bride) 850.00

Perhaps one of the most
beautiful dolls ever, *Wendy
Goes to the World's Fair,
1893*, was a very special
8in (20cm) doll made for
Shirley's Doll House.
Dolls of this quality make
collecting fun today and
offer high value tomorrow!

8" (20cm) hard plastic, first MADC doll, MADC Doll Club, 1989
(see Special Dolls)..$ 200.00
WENDY (FROM PETER PAN) 15" (38cm) hard plastic, 1953 ....650.00
14" (36cm) plastic, vinyl, 1969 ....300.00
8" (20cm) hard plastic, slippers with pom-poms, no faces, Storyland
Dolls, 1991-1993...55.00
WENDY ANGEL 8" (20cm) hard plastic, 1954 ....1200.00
WENDY ANN (see Alexander-Kins)
9" (23cm) composition, painted eyes, 1936-1940 ....325.00
11-15" (28-38cm) composition, 1935-1948.....................................500.00
14" (36cm) composition, in riding habit, 1938-1939 (some wigged).........400.00
17-21" (43-53cm) composition, 1938-1944 ....650.00-850.00
14½-17" (37-43cm) hard plastic, 1948-1949 ....850.00
16-22" (41-56cm) hard plastic, 1948-1950 ....850.00
23-25" (58-64cm) hard plastic, 1949 ....825.00
20" (51cm) hard plastic, 1956 ....525.00
WENDY GOES TO THE WORLD'S FAIR, 1893 8" (20cm), made for Shirley's
Doll House, 1993 (see Special Dolls) 80.00
WENDY HONORS THE MADAME 8" (20cm) hard plastic, mid-year release,
1993..100.00
WENDY LOVES BEING JUST LIKE MOMMY 1993 ....75.00

A real surprise and quite a jem, this 8in (20cm) *Shriner* was made for the Shriner's Convention in 1993 at San Antonio. Made for the Potentate's wives, very few will be offered for sale to collectors. It is fun to try and locate rarities for our collections!

WENDY "LOVES BEING LOVED" 8" (20cm) hard plastic doll and wardrobe, gift box, mid-year release, 1992 ....$ 105.00
WENDY LOVES FAO 8" (20cm) hard plastic, made for FAO Schwarz, 1993 (*see Special Dolls*) 70.00
WENDY LOVES HER ABC'S 8" (20cm) hard plastic, made for ABC Unlimited Productions, 1993 (*see Special Dolls*) 80.00
WENDY LOVES STORYLAND 8" (20cm) hard plastic, made for Neiman Marcus, 1993 (*see Special Dolls*) ....N/A
WENDY LOVES SUMMER 8" (20cm) hard plastic, box set, 1993 (doll and wardrobe)..80.00
WENDY LOVES SUN DRESS 8" (20cm) hard plastic, 1993 ....35.00
WENDY LOVES THE COUNTRY FAIR 8" (20cm) hard plastic, 1993 ....55.00
WHITE RABBIT cloth, felt, 1940s 500.00-600.00
WILSON, EDITH 5th set, First Ladies Series, 1988 ....85.00
WILSON, ELLEN 5th set, First Ladies Series, 1988 ....85.00
WINNIE WALKER 15" (38cm) hard plastic, 1953...245.00
18-23" (46-58cm) 375.00
In trunk, trousseau, 1953-1954 ....800.00
WINTER 14" (36cm) plastic, vinyl, Classic Dolls, 1993 ....150.00
WINTER SPORTS 8" (20cm) hard plastic, made for Shirley's Doll House, 1991 (*see Special Dolls*) 75.00
WINTER WONDERLAND 8" (20cm) hard plastic, made for Nashville Show, 1991 (*see Special Dolls*) 185.00
WINTER WONDERLAND II 8" (20cm) hard plastic, made for Nashville Show, 1992 (*see Special Dolls*) 95.00
WINTERTIME 8" (20cm) hard plastic, MADC Premiere, 1992 (*see Special Dolls*) 225.00
WITCH 8" (20cm) hard plastic, Americana Series, 1992 ....55.00
WITCH 8" (20cm) hard plastic, Americana Series, 1992-1993 ....55.00
WITHERS, JANE 12-13½" (31-34cm) composition, closed mouth, 1937 ....950.00
15-17" (38-43cm), 1937-1939 ....1200.00
17" (43cm) cloth body, 1939 ....1300.00
18-19" (46-48cm), 1937-1939 ....1300.00
19-20" (48-51cm), closed mouth version 1400.00
20-21" (51-53cm), 1937...1800.00
WYNKEN, BLYNKEN & NOD 8" (20cm) hard plastic, set of three dolls and a wooden shoe, Storyland Dolls, 1993 ....200.00

Y YOLANDA 12" (31cm) hard plastic, vinyl, slim teen-age body, 1965 (assorted outfits) 325.00
YUGOSLAVIA 8" (20cm) hard plastic, bend knee, 1968-1972 ....135.00
8" (20cm) straight leg, 1973-1975 ....60.00
8" (20cm) straight leg, 1976-1986 ....55.00
8" (20cm), CU Gathering, 1987 FAD (*see Special Dolls*) 125.00

Z ZORINA BALLERINA 17" (43cm) composition, 1937-1938................1200.00

Twenty Special Years of Special Dolls
Compiled by Benita Schwartz

YEAR	NAME OF DOLL & SIZE	PRODUCED FOR	OTHER INFORMATION
1972-1976	Alice 8" (20cm)	Disney	Bend Knee
1972-1976	Snow White 8" (20cm)	Disney	Bent Knee
1973	Tinkerbelle 8" (20cm)	Disney	Straight Leg
1980	The Enchanted Doll 8" (20cm)	EDH	LE of 3000, Lace Trim
1981	The Enchanted Doll 8" (20cm)	EDH	LE of 3423, Eyelet Trim
1983	Ballerina Trunk Set 8" (20cm)	EDH	Blue or Pink Tutu
1984	Ballerina 8" (20cm)	MADC Convention	FAD of 360 Dolls
1985	Cinderella & Trunk 14" (36cm)	EDH	Comes with Glass Slipper
1985	Happy Birthday Madame 8" (20cm)	MADC Convention	FAD of 450 Dolls
1986	Scarlett 8" (20cm)	MADC Convention	FAD of 625, Red Ribbon Trim
1987	Yugoslavia 8" (20cm)	CU Gathering	FAD
1987	Pussycat 18" (46cm)	FAO Schwarz	Pale Blue Dress & Bonnet
1987	Cowboy 8" (20cm)	MADC Convention	LE of 720 Dolls
1988	Miss Scarlett 14" (36cm)	Belk & Leggett	N/A
1988	Tippi 8" (20cm)	CU Gathering	LE of 800 Dolls
1988	The Enchanted Doll 10" (25cm)	EDH	LE of 5000 Dolls
1988	Brooke 14" (36cm)	FAO Schwarz	Blond eor Brunette Hair
1988	Flapper 10" (25cm)	MADC Convention	FAD of 720, Black Dress
1989	Rachel 8" (20cm)	Belk & Leggett	N/A
1989	Miss Leigh 8" (20cm)	CU Gathering	LE of 800 Dolls
1989	Cinderella 10" (25cm)	Disney	LE of 250 Dolls
1989	Sleeping Beauty 21" (53cm)	Disney Auction	One of a Kind
1989	Ballerina 8" (20cm)	EDH	LE of 360, Blue Tutu
1989	David & Diana 8" (20cm)	FAO Schwarz	Comes With Wagon
1989	Samantha 14" (36cm)	FAO Schwarz	N/A
1989	Southern Belle 10" (25cm)	My Doll House	Blonde or Brunette Hair
1989	Briar Rose 8" (20cm)	MADC Convention	LE of 804, Cissette Face

YEAR	NAME OF DOLL & SIZE	PRODUCED FOR	OTHER INFORMATION
1989	Jane Avril 10" (25cm)	Marshall Fields	N/A
1989	Wendy 8" (20cm)	MADC Club Doll	1st MADC Doll
1989	Noel 12" (31cm)	NECS	LE of 5000, Porcelain Doll
1989	Little Women 12" (31cm)	Sears	Set of 6 Dolls
1989	Victoria 14" (36cm)	Lord & Taylor	N/A
1990	Nancy Jean 8" (20cm)	Belk & Leggett	N/A
1990	Shea 8" (20cm)	CU Gathering	LE of 800 Dolls
1990	Snow White 12" (31cm)	Disney	LE of 750 Dolls
1990	Bobbie Sox 8" (20cm)	Disney	N/A
1990	Christine 21" (53cm)	Disney Auction	One of a Kind
1990	Vermont Maiden 8" (20cm)	EDH	LE of 3600, 2 Hair Colors
1990	Cissy By Scassi 21" (53cm)	FAO Schwarz	N/A
1990	Bessy Brooks Bride 8" (20cm)	Greenville Show	FAD of 200 Dolls
1990	Halloween 8" (20cm)	Greenville Show	FAD of 200 Dolls
1990	Cheerleader 8" (20cm)	I. Magnin	FAD, Letter "S" on Sweater
1990	Scarlett 8" (20cm)	MADC Symposium	FAD of 800 Dolls
1990	Riverboat Queen 8" (20cm)	MADC Convention	LE of 900 Dolls
1990	Polly Pigtails 8" (20cm)	MADC Club Doll	N/A
1990	Queen Elizabeth I 10" (25cm)	My Doll House	N/A
1990	Madame Butterfly 10" (25cm)	Marshall Fields	N/A
1990	Joy 12" (31cm)	NECS	LE of 5000, Porcelain Dolls
1990	Party Trunk 8" (20cm)	Neiman Marcus	N/A
1990	Angel Face 8" (20cm)	Shirley's Dollhouse	LE of 3500
1990	Beth 10" (25cm)	Spiegel	N/A
1990	Sailor Boy 8" (20cm)	UFDC Luncheon	LE of 260
1991	Cameo Lady 10" (25cm)	Collector's United	LE of 1000
1991	Winter Wonderland 8" (20cm)	Nashville Show	FAD of 200, Ice Skater
1991	Easter Bunny 8" (20cm)	A Child at Heart	LE of 3000, 3 Hair Colors
1991	Springtime 8" (20cm)	MADC Premier	LE of 1600 Dolls
1991	Sailor Boy 8" (20cm)	FAO Schwarz	N/A
1991	Fannie Elizabeth 8" (20cm)	Belk & Leggett	N/A
1991	Autumn in New York 10" (25cm)	NY Doll Club	FAD of 260
1991	Ring Master 8" (20cm)	CU Gathering	LE of 800 Dolls
1991	Queen Charlotte 10" (25cm)	MADC Convention	LE of 900 Dolls

YEAR	NAME OF DOLL & SIZE	PRODUCED FOR	OTHER INFORMATION
1991	Miss Liberty 10" (25cm)	MADC Club Doll	N/A
1991	Pandora 8" (20cm)	Dolls in Bearland	LE of Approximately 1800
1991	David, the Little Rabbi 8" (20cm)	Celia's Dolls	LE of 3600, 3 Hair Colors
1991	Mouseketeer 8" (20cm)	Disney	N/A
1991	Farmer's Daughter 8" (20cm)	EDH	LE of 4000, 3 Hair Colors
1991	Miss Magnin 10" (25cm)	I. Magnin	LE of 2500
1991	Empress Elisabeth 10" (25cm)	My Doll House	N/A
1991	Merry Angel 8" (20cm)	Spiegel	Christmas Tree Topper
1991	Miss Unity 10" (25cm)	UFDC Luncheon	LE of 310 Dolls
1991	Winter Sports 8" (20cm)	Shirley's Dollhouse	FAD of 975 Dolls
1991	Welcome Home 8" (20cm)	Mid-Year Release	2 Hair Colors, Boy or Girl, Black or White
1991	Camelot in Columbia 8" (20cm)	Columbia Show	FAD of 400 Dolls
1991	Carnevale 14" (36cm)	FAO Schwarz	N/A
1991	Beddy Bye Brooke 14" (36cm)	FAO Schwarz	N/A
1991	Little Huggums 12" (31cm)	Imaginarium	2 Hair Colors, Also Bald
1991	Alice and the White Rabbit 10" (25cm)	Disney	LE of 750 Dolls
1991	Queen Isabella 21" (53cm)	Disney Auction	One of a Kind
1991	Melody & Friend 8" (20cm) and 26" (66cm)	Gunzel	LE of 1000*
1992	Winter Wonderland II 8" (20cm)	Nashville Show	FAD of 200, Skier
1992	Wintertime 8" (20cm)	MADC Premiere	LE of 1650 Dolls
1992	Spring Break 8" (20cm)	Metroplex Show	LE of 400 Dolls
1992	Prom Queen 8" (20cm)	MADC Convention	LE of 1100 Dolls
1992	Faith 8" (20cm)	CU Gathering	LE of 800 Dolls
1992	Little Miss Godey 8" (20cm)	MADC Club Doll	N/A
1992	Round Up Day Mouseketeer 8" (20cm)	Disney	N/A
1992	Little Miss Magnin 8" (20cm)	I. Magnin	LE of 3600, 2 Hair Colors
1992	Little Huggum 12" (31cm)	I. Magnin	LE of 1500, Has Cradle
1992	Beddy-Bye Brooke & Brenda	FAO Schwarz	Matching 14" (36cm) & 8" (20cm) Pair
1992	Susannah 8" (20cm)	Dolly Dears	LE of 400 Dolls

YEAR	NAME OF DOLL & SIZE	PRODUCED FOR	OTHER INFORMATION
1992	Suellen 12" (31cm)	Jean's Dolls	FAD of 192, Blonde Hair
1992	My Little Sweetheart 8" (20cm)	A Child at Heart	LE of 4000, 4 Hair Colors
1992	My Little Sweetheart 8" (20cm)	A Child at Heart	LE of 500, Black Skin
1992	Annabelle 8" (20cm)	Belk & Leggett	LE of 3000 Dolls
1992	Mardi Gras 10" (25cm)	Spiegel	LE of 3000 Dolls
1992	Queen of Hearts 10" (25cm)	Disney	LE of 500 Dolls
1992	It's A Girl 21" (53cm)	Disney Auction	One-of-a-Kind
1992	Emperor & Nightingale**	Disney Auction	One-of-a-Kind
1992	Queen Elizabeth II 8" (20cm)	Mid-Year Release	N/A
1992	Wendy Loves Being Loved 8" (20cm)	Mid-Year Release	3 Hair Colors
1992	Alpine Christmas Twins 8" (20cm)	Christmas Shoppe	LE of 2000, 5 Hair Color Combinations
1992	Little Emperor 8" (20cm)	UFDC Luncheon	LE of 400 Dolls
1992	Le Petit Boudoir 10" (25cm)	Collector's United	LE of 700 Dolls
1992	Thoroughly Modern Wendy 8" (20cm)		Disney
1992	Joy Noel Tree Topper 10" (25cm)	Spiegel	LE of 3000 Dolls
1992	Bathing Beauty 10" (25cm)	UFDC Luncheon	LE of 300 Dolls
1992	Oktoberfest 8" (20cm)	Greenville Show	FAD of 200 Dolls
1992	Oktoberfest Boy 8" (20cm)	Greenville Show	FAD of 6 Dolls
1992	Courtney & Friends	Gunzel	LE of 1200 Dolls*
1992	Drucilla 14" (36cm)	MADC Convention	FAD of Approximately 250 Dolls
1992	Farmer's Daughter Goes to Town 8" (20cm)		EDH LE of 1600 Dolls, 3 Hair Colors

  * Doll Artist Hildegard Gunzel has created limited edition porcelain dolls. Some come with Madame Alexander Dolls. Melody's friend is an 8" (20cm) Wendy dressed to match. Courtney comes with two 8" (20cm) Alexander-kins, a boy and a girl, dressed in coordinating outfits.

  ** The Emperor and The Nightingale is a joint effort by Gund and the Alexander Doll Company. The Emperor is a Gund teddy bear dressed in an Oriental costume created by the Alexander Doll Company designers. The Nightingale is an 8" (20cm) Wendy doll.

The Alexander Doll Company
1993 Special Dolls

Anastasia 14" (36cm) — MADC Convention Special FAD
Bon Voyage Little Miss Magnin 8" (20cm) — I. Magnin
Bon Voyage Miss Magnin 10" (25cm) — I. Magnin
Caroline 8" (20cm) — Belk & Leggett
Cissy Bride 1921 21" (53cm) — Disneyland. One-of-a-Kind
   companions 8" (20cm) (2)
Columbian Sailor 12" (31cm) — UFDC Convention Luncheon
Diamond Lil 10" (25cm) — MADC Convention
Homecoming 8" (20cm) — 1993 MADC Premiere
Hope 8" (20cm) — CU Gathering
Jack Be Nimble 8" (20cm) — Dolly Dears
Little Miss Godey 8" (20cm) — MADC Club Doll
Monique 8" (20cm) — Disneyland
Pamela Plays Dress-Up at Grandma's 12" (31cm) — Horchow
Princess and the Pea 8" (20cm) — Dolly Dears
Saks Own Christmas Carol 8" (20cm) — Saks Fifth Ave
Snow White N/A — Disneyland
Texas Shriner 8" (20cm) — Shriners' National Convention, San Antonio

Trick and Treat 8" (20cm) pair — A Child at Heart
Wendy Goes to the World's Fair 8" (20cm) — Shirley's Doll House
Wendy Loves FAO 8" (20cm) — FAO Schwarz
Wendy Loves Her ABC's 8" (20cm) — ABC Unlimited Productions
Wendy Loves Storyland 8" (20cm) — Neiman Marcus

Other Distinguished Reference Books by the Author

Doll Fashion Anthology and Price Guide, 4th Revised Edition

This colorful book highlights over three decades of *Barbie®* favorites. American and International "fashion dolls" at their 1993 values are the focus of this book featuring 98 stunning color photographs out of 293 photographs. Includes such popular doll stars as Mattel's *Barbie®*, Ideal's *Tammy®* and American Character's *Tressy®*. 200 pages. 6" x 9". PB Item #H4679. $12.95

Contemporary Doll Stars

A special edition book containing Mr. Mandeville's most exclusive articles written for *Doll Reader®* magazine. The book is divided into four large sections: the 1950s, 1960s and 1970s, contemporary dolls and *Barbie®*. As a renowned expert and premiere dealer of modern dolls, Mr. Mandeville provides helpful insights into the world of doll collecting. Featured are 69 color photographs out of 363 photographs. 192 pages. 8½" x 11". PB. Item #H4380. $14.95

Golden Age of Collectible Dolls

Become reacquainted with these baby boomer dolls and the era of fashion reflected by these dolls. You will spot the favorite dolls of the 1950s and early 1960s in the 142 color and 57 b/w photos of such favorites as *Chatty Cathy®*, *Miss Curity*, *Barbie®*, *G.I. Joe®* and a host of others. An exquisite photo album ideal for any doll lover — now in its 2nd big printing! 144 pages. 8½" x 11". HB. Item #H3915. $25.00

Ginny...An American Toddler Doll, Revised Edition

The history of the popular *Ginny* dolls from her humble beginnings to now has been revised and updated to contain a new chapter about the Dakin Company's collectible *Ginny* dolls. Featured are 81 distinguishing color photographs of the dolls and their outfits as well as an updated price guide with the current market value of those sought after collectibles. 136 pages. 6" x 9". PB. Item #H4265. $12.95

2nd Ginny...Price Guide for An American Toddler Doll

A valuable companion to *Ginny...An American Toddler Doll* updates *Ginny* prices for 1991 plus *Ginny* doll photos in gorgeous color! An indispensable price guide for one of the most collectible dolls ever made! Features 10 color photographs. 24 pages. 6" x 9". PB. Item #H4264.

Other books include:
Kathe Kruse Price Guide
Celebrity Doll Price Guide and Annual, co-authored with John Axe

About the Author

Philadelphia based collector-dealer-author A. Glenn Mandeville is no stranger to the doll world.

"I have always been attracted to perfect miniature things," says Glenn.

As a teen-ager, this love translated into model trains, and later to dolls.

"The same elements exist in dolls and trains...the flawless miniaturization of life," is often quoted by the author.

In the mid-1980s Glenn began writing doll articles and books for Hobby House Press, Inc. At the time, he was the head of the foreign language department for a local school system. During the summer, he would prowl the flea markets for rare doll finds.

This hobby soon became a full time business. Serving as Regional Director for United Federation of Doll Clubs, Inc., and as the first Chairman of Judges, Modern Division, Glenn has left an indelible mark on the collector's world.

More books followed on collectible dolls, and Glenn became a frequent guest on the talk show circuit including CBS's "Regis & Kathie Lee," CNBC's "Smart Money," NBC's "Eddie Huggins," and the RKO Radio Network.

Glenn's personal appearances at leading doll shops and collector's gatherings led him to the Presidency of the Madame Alexander Doll Club for 1992.

"I can honestly say I was overwhelmed," says Glenn, when referring to the Madame Alexander Doll Club. "Collectors are really eager to learn the most that they can about their hobby."

It was the collector outreach that led Glenn to compile the Madame Alexander Dolls Value Guide.

"Shared knowledge is my goal," quotes Glenn, and as collectors agree, this book has it all!